WITHDRAWN

CANADA IN PEACE AND WAR

CANADA
IN PEACE AND WAR

EIGHT STUDIES IN
NATIONAL TRENDS SINCE 1914

Edited by

CHESTER MARTIN

OXFORD UNIVERSITY PRESS
LONDON   TORONTO   NEW YORK
1941

Issued under the auspices of the
Canadian Institute of International Affairs

COPYRIGHT, 1941
by OXFORD UNIVERSITY PRESS
First published, January 1941

Printed in Canada

FOREWORD

I

THE peril which now confronts the whole English-speaking world will make it increasingly difficult to record the trends of the last quarter of a century in Canada with precision or detachment. The Nazi assault has now reached the citadel of our way of life, and few realists will now be found to rely upon Maginot lines either of defence or of thought.

This attempt to interpret some of the most significant of these trends was originally made under other auspices[1] at a time when the French Republic and even the little democracies of Europe appeared as yet to be as secure as many still seem to think the great republic and the smaller democracies in this hemisphere. Without sharing either of these delusions, the attempt has been made to preserve the original objectivity of these studies. In one sense it was almost as hard to be a realist in February 1940, during the deceptive calm before the zero hour of the war, as it has since become in the midst of war to interpret the trends of peace. Already there were signs foreshadowing the 'dark days' of 1940, when civilization was to come

[1] A series of lectures (February and March, 1940) by the Departments of Political Economy and Modern History at the University of Toronto. The opening lecture of the series was introduced by Dr. H. J. Cody, President of the University.

nearer, it may be, to eclipse than at any other pass in modern history. But these portents, even for the most resolute realist in February 1940, could scarcely have equalled the perils of reality. The importance of realism in the present crisis must be equally obvious, for without the hard facts of the past two decades it would be impossible either to take stock of the present or to plan for the future. In value, therefore, as well as in permanent interest, this survey of the last quarter-century in Canada ought to gain rather than lose by the measure of detachment that was still possible while as yet the evil days had come not. At any rate, its value, for whatever it is worth, would not be increased now by trying to transplant it from one geological age to another.

The deductions which may be drawn from some of these studies and from unforeseen trends since set in motion by the unpredictable train of events, may be another matter, for it must surely be obvious that the speed and momentum of the present emergency may require a new daring in addition to all the old sagacity and courage of the past. As late as the time of Elizabeth men were still writing treatises to prove that the long-bow could hold its own with gunpowder. The form of things to come if the Anglo-American world as we have known it is to survive may require, in the realm of air and sea power and international trade, for instance, a political daring as revolutionary for our day as Drake and his 'blue-water school' ever ventured in the naval strategy of the sixteenth century. In these circumstances trends may be transformed almost over night into crises; for the cloud which was no larger than a man's hand in February 1940, has since darkened the whole sky. The lease of air and naval bases to the United States and the Canadian counterpart to this development, the work of the Canadian-American permanent joint board on defence—appointed on August 22 as a result of the Ogdensburg agreement of August 17—may mark a trend in world history. 'In ultimate importance', said Mr. King a few days ago, 'it far surpasses the formation of the triple Axis' of Germany, Italy, and Japan; and the 'close harmony' which Mr. Churchill himself foreshadowed in announcing the British decision ('spontaneously and without being asked or offered any inducement') may be a prodigious portent for the Canadian people.

II

In one respect at least this crisis may be expected to simplify rather than complicate some of the trends outlined in these studies. The traditional rôle of Canada as an interpreter between Great Britain and the United States has been honoured in the breach rather than in the observance so long as latent antipathies and prejudices have been allowed to play upon the relations between them: so long too as the Dominion found it necessary to run the gauntlet between them in pursuit of a modest nationhood of its own. Many of these tendencies are now obsolete, and the function of the Dominion *vis-à-vis* the United States on the one hand and Great Britain on the other may be endowed by events with an importance not at all of our seeking.

The only American nation to take arms against German Nazidom declared war on September 10,

1939, by an act as deliberate and autonomous as the declaration of the United States in 1917. This functioning of nationhood has now become a commonplace in Canada, but it has been profoundly misunderstood, at various stages of its development, by many both in Great Britain and the United States who long persisted in regarding it as a movement towards or away from one or the other of these two historic branches of the English-speaking world. Canadians who know well enough that it was nothing of the sort may be pardoned for trying to appraise these trends a little more discerningly at this crisis in their history. It is only by transcending traditional antipathies, both British and American, in a national destiny sanctioned by both, that Canada, in these difficult days that lie ahead, can hope to make a modest contribution of its own to mutual co-operation and goodwill; and the time may be coming for more assertive action if those things which we all have in common are to survive.

But the gravest trends in either peace or war for Canada are those of recent months which concern the survival of Britain as the bulwark of our own freedom. Since these studies were completed in their original form the whole world has gone far towards that 'descent into a new and terrible barbarism' which the Prime Minister of Canada deprecated at the beginning of the war. The subjugation of one after another of the little democracies of Europe followed by the collapse of the French Republic has left Britain and Switzerland once again as the historic haunts of freedom in Europe—the same 'two voices . . . one of the mountains, one of the sea', which Wordsworth invoked against the domination of Napoleon. During the 'dark days' of 1940 the nations of the British Commonwealth have been standing almost literally alone in arms against a new and devastating 'world order'.

No student of sea power as expounded so brilliantly in the United States by the late Captain Mahan can mistake the implications of that doctrine for this Dominion. The function of sea power for a century has been to ensure free access to the seven seas for peaceful commerce; and that is to be kept, by Britain or by any other power, only by carrying sea power to the utmost confines of the sea, not by hovering defensively on the confines of the land. If British sea power in the North Sea or at the gateways of the Mediterranean is destroyed, or by a device similar to Hitler's frustrated design for the French navy, transferred to the enemy, the control not only of European waters and the east Atlantic but of world commerce would pass to the totalitarian powers of Europe. No Maginot line of the Atlantic Ocean or any other tactics of defence on this side of the Atlantic could then safeguard the world commerce of free nations or the shores of Canada herself against a power which is already dominant from the Baltic to the Bay of Biscay. By every basic principle of the 'blue-water school' which has prevailed in naval strategy since the days of Drake and Blake and Nelson, the place to defend Canada would seem to be in the North Sea and the Mediterranean. Conversely, the combination of sea power and supremacy in the air would be not twice but four or five times as formidable as either one without the other. The courage of Britain during these 'dark days' has been more than the survival of an indomitable tradition; and the Commonwealth Air Training Plan may well be the most constructive contribution yet undertaken in Canada for the defence of freedom on this continent.

It may not be too soon, also, to scrutinize a subtler menace which has proved scarcely less successful than tanks and dive bombers in the subjugation of every democracy beneath the Nazi yoke. It has already appeared openly in this hemisphere, and this particular type of fifth column may not be without a bearing upon the future of this continent. Those who are prepared to resign themselves to a Nazified Europe would be the first to advocate the Nazification of this hemisphere in a dozen aspects of its economy and government, to permit the one to do business with the other in a cynical and soulless partnership. In Canada and the United States, to be sure, it would be necessary to rewrite Magna Carta and the Bill of Rights and the Declaration of Independence and the Gettysburg speech of Abraham Lincoln—or at least to purvey them as mere rhetorical verbiage to a recreant people— before these two kindred nations could fit into this pattern; but predatory interests have fewer loyalties than those who hold the 'simple faiths of freedom, truth, and justice'. With this insidious economic appeal for the 'new order' in Europe has been combined the subtlest propaganda of our day, a technique which relies not upon direct propaganda or counter-propaganda but upon propaganda against any form of propaganda whatever, particularly the truth, in the hope that great masses of people can be backed up into a corner, a sort of moral paralysis, in which it will be impossible for them to face up to moral conviction in any form. This in itself is an alarming circumstance, for nothing is more appalling in the achievements of the totalitarian technique during the last ten years than the systematic sabotage of the old order in moral values. A resurrection of these imponderables is long overdue if this black death is ever to be stayed. It is possible that in Canada as elsewhere the basic principles of our way of life must yet be tried as by fire before Canadian nationhood can hope to emerge into a lasting and worthy rôle in the Anglo-American world.

III

The subject matter and form of these studies may require brief comment. Originating in a series of lectures which followed an earlier series on the causes and immediate background of the war, these eight themes have retained as far as possible their original content with a minimum of change in the form of foot-notes and other *impedimenta* of formal scholarship. A measure of integration will be obvious in the topics selected for discussion but no attempt has been made to give the series as a whole what Mill once called 'a false air of nice adjustment'. The reverse, in fact, would be nearer to the truth. Each of the contributors was already engaged upon some aspect of Canadian national development, and it was deemed wiser to appropriate this varied range of material ready-made, rather than to affect a more systematic coverage of Canadian development in all its aspects during these years of war and peace and war again since 1914.

By chance, however, rather than by design a somewhat remarkable degree of integration was found to be possible. The introductory study, a survey of recent 'Trends in Canadian Nationhood', distinguished more than one ingredient which was to find a place in greater detail in subsequent studies of the series; and the culmination of Canadian nationhood in the declaration of war on September 10, 1939, was an appropriate prelude to its function and to its stake in the present conflict. Professor Creighton's study of 'Federal Relations in Canada since 1914' was a fitting corollary to the part which he had already taken in the preparation of material for the Rowell-Sirois Commission.[1] The quickening of federal functions during the last war, followed during the post-war years by renewed social and economic crises and the steady deterioration in federal powers of dealing with them, culminated in 1937 in wholesale disallowance of federal legislation by the Judicial Committee of the Privy Council, and brought an impasse from which escape was sought in the Rowell-Sirois Commission. For the findings of the Commission, here outlined, Professor Creighton bespeaks a broad-minded consideration. 'The new Fathers of Confederation have performed a creative act comparable to that of the Quebec Conference and in harmony with its guiding principles.'

The third study of the series, a masterly survey of economic trends by Professor Innis, reaches conclusions which many Canadians will find not only impressive but disquieting. With characteristic caution, however, the evidence is left to speak for itself, and the modest verdict of 'the new priesthood'—the economists

---

[1] *Royal Commission on Dominion-Provincial Relations,* Appendix 2: 'British North America at Confederation', pp. 104.

whose voices are 'heard throughout the land'—is rendered in the humour of Belloc's immortal couplet:

> They answered as they took their fees
> There is no cure for this disease.

The closing note of Dr. Innis's study is the Canadian tradition 'of neither accepting nor imposing domination. Only in such a world could we of all countries have lived and only in such a world can we live.'

In the fourth study, on 'Population Problems and Policies', Professor Bladen discusses another disquieting aspect of Canadian development—the trends of European, American, and Canadian demography. Rooted as this problem appears to be in prevailing world conditions rather than in isolated or sporadic policies, it is found to contain for Canada baffling factors of staple production, of race fertility, and of immigration. 'With an economy geared to export trade', and with the optimum rate of growth for Canada therefore 'dependent on factors outside Canada', projects for large-scale immigration are found to be less attractive than a policy of 'reducing mortality and increasing fertility at home.'

In the fifth and sixth studies of the series will be found a survey of Canada's first war effort from 1914 to the Peace Treaty and of the slowly evolving pattern of Canada's external relations. In 'Canada and the Last War' Professor Underhill has presented a stirring summary of his earlier narrative 'The Canadian Forces in the War' in *The Empire at War* (vol. ii), edited by the late Sir Charles Lucas of the Colonial Office. The Canadian Corps 'set up a record of continuous victory that was unsurpassed and indeed unequalled among all the troops on the western front'; and the story of the Imperial Munitions Board under the chairmanship of Sir Joseph Flavelle was the 'greatest romance in Canadian industrial history.' It spent 1250 million dollars, and in 1917 nearly a third of the shells fired from British guns on the western front were made in Canada. In 'Canadian External Relations' Professor Glazebrook has traced trends in Canadian policy which will be found in greater detail and in a broader context in his forthcoming volume on the history of the external relations of Canada. Canada declined European obligations at Locarno and Chanaq but accepted them, with implications which can scarcely yet be measured, in 1914 and 1939. In the interval 'we have been opportunists, hoping for the best, not always preparing for the worst.'

The two remaining studies—one a highly specialized analysis of certain constitutional trends in British and Canadian war-time technique and the other a synthesis of broader political trends in the Dominions of the British Commonwealth—were contributed somewhat reluctantly for publication on the plea that one was too narrow and the other too broad for a strictly Canadian scene. The authors of both however have been fairly overborne in this matter by the other contributors to the series and by the course of events. The timeliness of both these studies will now be self-evident. No phase of parliamentary government during the last war was more significant than the flexibility of the cabinet system in Great Britain and the Dominions in permitting the evolution of 'war cabinets', absolved from departmental and parliamentary routine in order to develop speed and incisiveness in war administration. In his study of 'Canadian and Imperial War Cabinets' Professor Dawson has traced these trends in the first world war and questioned the failure in the present conflict to utilize such well-tried expedients as parliamentary under-secretaries, a more efficient technique of cabinet business, and above all some device like the old Imperial War Cabinet through which Canadian views on war policy can be registered and interpreted. The appropriateness of this study will require no further vindication than the press-reports and discussion which followed Professor Dawson's original lecture. Professor Brady's penetrating study also—'Democracy in the Overseas Dominions'—has already been endowed by events with a poignancy and timeliness altogether unforeseen; for these communities which had scarcely emerged from adolescence during the last world war are now senior partners in a Commonwealth which has been holding the pass almost alone in arms against a ruthless and predatory 'world order'. 'If British sea power was destroyed as a consequence of the present war' these promising democratic experiments might pass away, for 'few countries will respond more quickly to the course of world history.'

Two observations may be added with regard to the series as a whole. It is obvious that many significant aspects of Canadian development have had to be omitted, and it will be equally obvious that uniformity of view is neither sought nor implied in those aspects which have been selected for review. Conspicuously omitted have been the trends in party politics, many vital problems of race and social adjustment, and more than one haunting problem of the 'imponderables' in

the morale of the Dominion; though passing references
to these will be found in the discussion of other issues.
Diversity of view or of emphasis is more easily vindicated. If consistency, as Emerson once said, is 'the
hobgoblin of little minds', there could be no more
ominous symptom for a series of studies like this than
a striving for meticulous consistency. A member of
the 'Apostles' at Cambridge once attributed the lassi-
tude through which that famous club appeared for a
time to be passing, to 'too much brotherly love': there
was not enough difference of opinion to engender
energetic action. Without these stimulating differences
of opinion it would be hard to account for the congenial
association of the two departments whose co-operation
is responsible for these studies of Canada in peace and
war.

By the same token each contributor must be absolved
from all opinions but his own. From the editor it may
be that other contributors are entitled to special abso-
lution. A joint obligation, shared deeply by all of
them, must be acknowledged to the Canadian Institute
of International Affairs under whose auspices this little
volume goes to press; and a special acknowledgment is
due from the editor for permission to publish his introductory study of 'Trends in Canadian Nationhood' in
the series of *Oxford Pamphlets on World Affairs*. And
finally a word must be added about the reluctant
decision to forgo an index. It was found that the eight
studies of the series were so nearly self-contained that
almost a completely new set of index-topics would be
required for each. In these circumstances a reader
would be almost as near the topic of his search in the
text of a particular study as he might find himself in

an index that was comprehensive enough to include them all. On one point at least the contributors were all agreed: a wilderness of page-numbers without topical references would have been worse than no index at all.

C. M.

University of Toronto,
November 16, 1940.

CONTENTS

CANADA IN PEACE AND WAR

I. TRENDS IN CANADIAN NATIONHOOD
by CHESTER MARTIN

I

SINCE early September, 1939, two functions of
Canadian nationhood have had momentous consequences. In one of them, perhaps the gravest ever
exercised by a responsible minister in this country, a
state of war between Canada and Germany was
proclaimed by the King on the advice of a Canadian
Prime Minister. In the other, the Minister of Finance
forecast a war expenditure for the first year of the war
more than five times the total amount of cash
subsidies and government loans advanced by the
government of Canada for the building of the Canadian Pacific Railway. Three weeks later the Prime
Minister announced the details of a Commonwealth
Air Training Plan which 'may well mean (I am quoting
from Mr. King's broadcast) that the final victory will
be shaped on Canadian soil.'

This is not the first time that these two phenomena,
autonomy and co-operation, have appeared together
in Canadian history; nor is it the first time that these
two trends, apparently so divergent, have been misread
by uninitiated observers. An Austrian minister has
recorded in the French press the prediction by Herr
Hitler to Chancellor von Schuschnigg that the British

Dominions would not again participate in another war, and that in the event of war the breakup of the British Commonwealth was altogether probable. Nearly six months before the Canadian declaration of war a reply was made (April, 1939) to that forecast: happily by the Hon. Mr. Lapointe, whose name, not so many years ago, was chiefly associated in English-speaking Canada, I suppose, with the Halibut Treaty and other technical aspects of autonomy. Neutrality in such a conflict as this, said Mr. Lapointe, would mean a civil war in Canada. 'We will resist all attempts to break up the Commonwealth, and if any dictator in the world has made up his mind that the British Commonwealth is going to be disrupted, he is basing his future projects on an absolute fallacy.'

Now this surely is a very remarkable circumstance. How can these two trends, so divergent in appearance, be so similar in practice? Can it be that they are but two aspects of the same thing? It would be folly, I think, to assume that they are so automatically, for Eire is a demonstration to the contrary in vindicating its right to neutrality in this war. Canada, however, has come to national maturity under happier auspices, for I cannot help thinking that certain trends in Canadian nationhood are much older and much stronger than they look, and that they are now rounding into something like an historical cycle.

For Canada and the other British Dominions nationhood has come by a very curious process: a process which is unique, if I am not mistaken, among the nations of the modern world. Britain herself, set apart by her insularity and a happy concourse of peoples nearly a thousand years ago, could boast a national spirit at a time when the medieval world still reflected something of the universality of imperial Rome. The Netherlands were moulded into nationhood in the crucible of successful revolt, almost exactly two centuries before the independence of the United States. Others like Italy or Germany have crystallized about a dominant nucleus. Like measles in adult life, nationality so long deferred is apt to develop awkward symptoms. At a time when science and civilization alike seemed to prescribe an era of integration for the modern world, nationalism in Germany has reverted to its crudest and most ruthless form. The nationhood which functions today in Canada is based upon a vastly different tradition—a tradition that can scarcely fail to have an abiding influence upon its temper and its function. John Morley once made the whimsical reflection 'how curious it is to see how exactly people follow their own characters all through life.' To divorce a nation from its history is about as feasible as divorcing an individual from his character; and it will be strange indeed if Canadian nationhood in world politics does not remain characteristically Canadian.

The development of nationhood in Canada is most clearly measurable, I am inclined to think, by comparison with that of our great neighbour. Beginning from the same colonial origins in a North American environment (though at vastly different stages of development) one took the high road of revolution and isolation, the other took the low road of evolution and association. Both have now completed cycles of remarkable similarity, but while Canada assuredly did not reach nationhood first, she has reached it in the end by a process which is much nearer to an international world order. In both cases it is possible, it seems to me, to distinguish four basic factors in the process, but with such differences in sequence and tempo and association that the whole gamut of peace and war now lies between them.

In the United States these four basic factors were all attempted by a single generation within less than a single decade. Full self-government was a corollary of political independence. Union was the product of revolution confirmed by one of the great constructive achievements of modern statesmanship, the constitution of 1787—though it required a civil war three-quarters of a century later to safeguard and preserve that union. Nationhood in international relations began to function almost automatically in defiance of one European power and with the aid of two others; but nearly a whole century of antipathies supervened between Britain and the United States as the republic turned deliberately from European entanglements to attack a much more lucrative and immediate task, the conquest and settlement of half a continent. This fourth factor was perhaps the greatest single ingredient in the unity and expansion of the republic, for almost every major aspect of policy was conditioned by it. The public domain of the United States, created when the original states of the union dedicated to the national government their conflicting claims to the hinterlands, was enlarged by purchase, by conquest, and diplomacy, from the Alleghany Mountains to Alaska in the span of eighty years. This fight for an expanding frontier was the background for the great transcontinentals, for the civil war itself, and for the widest range of land settlement ever directed by one government. With the completion of this task twenty or twenty-five years ago, the gates were barred to immigration, and a new set of problems has been slowly emerging in the United States—the establishment of a stable society and a stable economy on this continent, and another equally prodigious experiment, whether the greatest aggregation of population, wealth, and resources under one government in the world can remain isolated and insulated from a world in which freedom, as we understand it, is now fighting for its life.

In Canada these same four factors have conditioned the development of nationhood, but they have appeared in a different order, one at a time, and with long intervals between. The associations that attended the process have resulted in a vastly different tradition, and there is a vastly different outlook at the end.

Self-government, though implanted in the primitive legislation of colonial assemblies, began to function in administration only with what we call responsible government in 1848—the beginning of a long process which has come to include many of the attributes of nationhood only in our own day. Union of the British provinces was the work of the next generation, and now after seventy-five years—the stage marked by civil war in the United States—the growing-pains of Canadian federalism are still with us. Expansion to the Pacific was undertaken long before the young Dominion was ready for it. Here too the settlement of the frontier under federal auspices has formed a cycle of Canadian development—a cycle like that of the United States now rounding into completion in our own day. The functioning of Canada in international affairs has come last of all, and perhaps most rapidly of all, but anybody who is surprised at it must be singularly blind to the trends in Canadian self-government for more than ninety years.

During the last quarter of a century of war and peace and war again—the period here particularly under review—all four of these basic factors in Canadian nationhood have passed through some very notable changes. The best that one can hope to do in so brief a survey is to illustrate a few of these trends; but one general remark might be in order at the outset.

To many observers the appearance of Canada in the apparel of nationhood at the close of the last war seemed so sudden and so spectacular that an explanation was sought in the consequences of the war itself. The title of a brilliant study by Professor Elliott of Harvard was *The New British Empire*; and even Sir Alfred Zimmern has suggested the term 'Third British Empire' for the period after 1914. For Canadians themselves these abrupt and sudden transitions are almost meaningless. The watershed to nationhood for Canada was passed ninety years ago in the achievement of what we call in Canada 'responsible government'. The principles of its growth were applied at first, it is true, to issues of purely local interest, and even Lord Durham, as we all know, conceived it possible to withhold from their operation the whole range of foreign policy and trade, defence, crown lands and the very form of the constitution. Elgin saw much more clearly that these artificial distinctions were impossible. From beginning to end the range of responsible government was to be determined by one thing and one thing only—the legitimate interests of the Canadian people. With the expansion of those interests, one field after another was subjected to the same stringent responsibility until all the attributes of nationhood have now been brought within its scope. When the legitimate interests of the Canadian people crossed—irretraceably as it seems to me—the boundaries of the Dominion into world politics in 1914 a dozen new aspects of self-government were added to the forty or fifty already encompassed since 1848. In Sir Arthur Currie's command in the last war, in the participation of Sir Robert Borden and his colleagues in the peace treaty, in Canada's membership in the League of Nations, in the election of Canada to the Council of the League in 1927—in these and a score of other incidents there is to be seen a consistent trend of practice. What has changed is not the old principle but the scope of its application. New responsibilities have been assumed, one at a time, each in the order of its importance, each as the Dominion was ready for it. I once suggested in the United States that Canada has developed to full nationhood by a process of *incubation*. Measured by the standards of September 10, 1939, the ideas which Robert Baldwin tried so solemnly to impress upon Lord Durham in this city almost exactly a hundred years ago look like 'primordial protoplasm'. Their sheltered growth, however, has been the most distinctive aspect of our history, and the young bird has now taken to the air with a vengeance.

II

The factor in Canadian nationhood which I have called self-government has already, I imagine, the remotest interest of all at the present time. Scarcely a decade and a half has passed since we were still wrangling about status and autonomy, and already the phrases come back like echoes from another world. It was only in 1923 that one of the most important of Imperial Conferences seriously began the patient work of regularizing the anomalies that still survived from the long era of incubation. More important in many respects than the more spectacular conferences of 1926 and 1930, the Imperial Conference of 1923 developed a very clear sense of direction which the later conferences merely confirmed. Most of these anomalies were removable by the age-old technique of unwritten convention or usage—the most useful of all the expedients of British constitutional development. By this technique the Crown had reached its present sanctuary in Great Britain. By this also the position of the Governor-General in Canada has been made to conform to that of the Crown in Great Britain. It was only the other day that the Governor-General ceased to be an appointee of the Colonial Office and became the personal representative of the Crown on the advice of Canadian ministers. Lord Bessborough's commission was signed 'By His Majesty's Command, R. B. Bennett' (March 20, 1931). A few months ago the King and Queen of Canada, in a gesture of statesmanship that can scarcely yet be calculated, discharged here the functions of their royal office in person. One of these has been described by an American observer as the 'personification of a thousand gracious decencies in public life', and the new Prime Minister of Quebec referred the other day to these imponderables as the event of the year in the unification of the Dominion.

A few of the old vestigial anomalies were based upon statutes and were therefore removable only by statutory enactment.[1] These were dealt with in the *Statute of Westminster*, 1931, 22 Geo. V, c. 4. A few anomalies of both sorts—based upon convention on the one hand and statute on the other—still remain. One was retained in the *Statute of Westminster* itself at the express stipulation of Canada because we have been unable to devise a more convenient method of amending the *B. N. A. Acts* than another Act of the British Parliament. In effect however the historic principle, evolved in practice over so many years and expressly formulated at the Imperial Conference of 1926, is now an accomplished fact. Great Britain and the Dominions are now 'in no way subordinate one to another in any aspect of their domestic or external affairs'. Characteristic of the same historic formula is the addition, in the same sentence, of free association and a 'common allegiance'. The mechanics of subordination have been supplanted by 'broad loyalties, by (the) common feelings and interests—in many cases, of history—and by devotion to great world ideals of peace and freedom.' 'That is the bond,' added Lord Balfour. 'If that is not enough nothing else is enough.' The most recent official pronouncement in Canada upon that point was made by the Hon. Mr. Lapointe himself as Minister of Justice (March 31): 'The Statute of Westminster, instead of being an agency of

---

[1] *Colonial Laws Validity Act* of 1865, *Merchant Shipping Act* of 1894, *Colonial Courts of Admiralty Act*, 1890, etc.

division, is an agency of unity, unity in liberty, without which no British nation can exist. . . . We will resist all attempts to break up the Commonwealth.' I venture to add a sentence spoken by the King himself in Canada: 'Even in this age of machines and mass production, the strength of human feeling is still the most potent of all the factors in world affairs.' Those who would interpret this subtle and dynamic philosophy in terms of the sentimental colonialism of the old order must be curiously blind to its true meaning in the developments of the last thirty years. Let an equally valid corollary be added, that when we cease to value and to defend our own freedom we are destroying the surest bond of the Commonwealth, the vital 'contexture (as Burke once called it) of this mysterious whole'. 'All this I know well enough', he added, 'will sound wild and chimerical to . . . those vulgar and mechanical politicians . . . who think that nothing exists but what is gross and material. . . . But to men truly initiated and rightly taught, these ruling and master principles . . . are in truth everything, and all in all.'

In tracing this trend of Canadian nationhood I have made no attempt to explore or even to list the score or so of attendant controversies, but one is tempted to add one general reflection with regard to them. While most of the wrangling has been done by the jurists and philosophers with their 'metaphysical distinctions', the real work has been done by practical statesmen relying upon empirical adjustments, reached, upon the whole, in a spirit of mutual forbearance. The truth is that there has not been a prime minister since Confederation who has not added to the stature of Canadian nationhood. The other day General Smuts in South Africa dropped the word sovereignty without the flicker of an eye-lash. A few days later Mr. Crerar, the least demonstrative of men, used it again in describing by radio from London the war effort of the Canadian people. 'No constraint from any source', he added, 'was placed upon us. Our action was entirely voluntary and our effort ... will be exerted to the maximum of the power of the Canadian people. May I add further that among the Canadian people as a whole there is a unity of spirit and determination of purpose that has never been surpassed on any issue that has ever come before them.' This, it will be conceded, is sovereignty of a new sort—not the introverted indefeasible sovereignty of the Austinian theory but sovereign association in a world where freedom in isolation is rapidly becoming obsolete. The only man in a free country who is a sovereign law unto himself these days is the gangster, and even gangsters have been known to associate for their own nefarious purposes.

III

The second major factor I have mentioned in Canadian nationhood, the union of the scattered British provinces into a transcontinental Dominion, has passed through many vicissitudes since 1914. I have no intention of trying to explore here the internal stresses and strains of Canadian federalism which have been under review for many months now by the Rowell Commission, and which will form the subject of the second lecture in this series by Professor Creighton. I have an idea that Professor Creighton's outlook may be more sombre than my own, for I cannot help reflecting upon the more desperate emergencies of other days—the crisis which brought even Brown and Macdonald together in 1864, the desperate venture of expansion to the Pacific from 1869 to 1871, the despair of the late eighties and early nineties when not only the defeatists of that day but a few of the 'Canada firsters' themselves were almost ready to strike their flag. The seventy-sixth anniversary of the Constitution of the United States was commemorated by the guns of Gettysburg to determine whether a nation so conceived and so dedicated could long endure. After all we have had no civil war in Canada, and the seventy-sixth anniversary of the Quebec Conference finds the Dominion united (perhaps as never before) in the face of an emergency which many thoughtful Canadians a few years ago predicted would break Confederation to pieces.

Twenty-five years ago the sisterhood of provinces in the Canadian federation had scarcely been completed. Alberta and Saskatchewan, though created provinces in 1905, were still like the old Province of Manitoba under federal administration in respect of their public lands. It was only in 1912 that Manitoba, Ontario, and Quebec were enlarged to their present boundaries. Meanwhile a long series of leading cases before the Judicial Committee of the Privy Council since Lord Watson's day, and a long series of semi-judicial political issues like the Ontario-Manitoba boundary dispute and the Manitoba School Question seemed to leave the advocates of provincial rights in full possession of the field. Co-operation began again (particularly in the fiscal field) during the last war as it has begun again in this; and though many of the old controversies were resumed after the war, there were signs, for a time, of magnanimity and of real courage that have not always been conspicuous in more recent years. Two illustrations may be cited without concealing at the same time the symptoms of less seemly controversy. The Natural Resources Question of the Prairie Provinces—an issue in provincial politics since 1880—was attacked by the federal government, both Conservative and Liberal, with real statesmanship,[1] and I venture to add that it was settled at last in 1930 in that spirit. The spirit too in which the Dominion implemented the terms of the Duncan Report on the Maritime Provinces in 1927— the sixtieth anniversary of Confederation—was worthy of the best traditions in Canadian history.

The descent into Avernus of two or three years ago is still fresh in our minds, and it is impossible to recall some of those passages in federal and provincial relations with complacency. But much of the strain, surely, was due to unprecedented and let us hope temporary shifts in the staple production of Canada. The drought in the West was the most prolonged and disastrous on record, but even pessimism cannot

[1] Norris to Meighen, December 15, 1920: 'The Prairie Provinces are not without pride in having been able to lend, so to speak, to the Dominion, the immediate resources without which these great national enterprises (railways and settlement) could never have been effected.'

In distinction to the usage with the other provinces of Confederation in section 109 of the *B. N. A. Act of* 1867, the Dominion in admitting Manitoba, Saskatchewan, and Alberta into federation in 1870 and 1905 determined to retain control of their public lands and administer them 'for the purposes of the Dominion' in the interests of rapid railway construction and settlement. What were left of the public lands in 1930 were returned to the Prairie Provinces, with compensation for those alienated for the purposes of the Dominion.

destroy the law of averages. Whatever the state of world markets, the productivity of the West is still unimpaired, and the crop of 1939 was the fifth largest on record. Meanwhile Saskatchewan which had supplied a domestic market for Canadian industry by producing more than $500,000,000 a year in agricultural wealth for more than a decade, was supplanted in the economy of the central provinces by the phenomenal development of mining within their own boundaries. Under the stimulus of war production and the improving prospects of the St. Lawrence system, a still further industrial development from the Great Lakes to the sea may well assume the proportions of a national trend towards a region already self-centred in the Canadian economy. This may be a much less cautious forecast than you are likely to get from Professor Innis in the third lecture of this series, but whatever these shifts in the Canadian economy it will be conceded that they have been and are likely to be reflected in recurring crises in the functioning of Canadian federalism. Curious that war should be so much more efficacious than peace in commanding the resourcefulness and public spirit of democracy.

Let me avow a national creed for Canada in defiance of the maladjustments of recent years. The Canadian federation, in its original conception and in its initial achievement, was the strongest among the true federations of the modern world—that is to say the federal powers by comparison with the provincial or state powers were much stronger in Canada than in the United States or Brazil or Australia. This was achieved discerningly by utilizing to the utmost the pressure under which Confederation had to be carried. Not only were residuary powers reserved for the federal government but by the powers specifically divided the national government was deliberately endowed with functions in taxation, in military and naval control, in trade and commerce, in transportation, and in finance, that would make armed secession like that in the United States forever impossible. Even 'property and civil rights', the most comprehensive of provincial rights under section 92 of the *B. N. A. Act of 1867*, were intended to gravitate towards the national government, and indeed the machinery for this in section 94 of the Act is standing there to this day discarded and rusty and unused:

The Parliament of Canada may make provisions for the uniformity of all or any of the laws relative to property and civil rights in Ontario, Nova Scotia, and New Brunswick, and of the procedure of all or any of the Courts in those three Provinces; and from and after the passing of any Act in that behalf the power of the Parliament of Canada to make laws in relation to any matter comprised in any such Act shall . . . be unrestricted; but any Act of the Parliament of Canada making provision for such uniformity shall not have effect in any Province unless and until it is adopted and enacted as law by the Legislature thereof.

It has been the opinion of both Mr. Cahan and Mr. Lapointe—Ministers of Justice in both Conservative and Liberal governments—that the action of the Judicial Committee of the Privy Council in reversing the demonstrable designs of the fathers of Confederation has been unfortunate and ought to be reversed. It is curious that the federal powers of the United States which began much weaker than those of the Dominion have been steadily reinforced by the

Supreme Court, while those of Canada, beginning with so wide a margin, have been impaired by the Judicial Committee of the Privy Council to the point where social legislation on a national scale is open to flagrant obstruction. Perhaps both trends may be interpreted as attempts to readjust the ballast, so to speak, of national lading, one weighted in favour of federal, the other in favour of state powers. More devastating perhaps than judicial interpretation in Canada have been the infirmities of political temper in exploiting differences instead of attacking their common problems by concurrent legislation. A national creed for Canada must begin with a dedication to the best rather than the worst in Canadian politics. I believe that there are resources of national spirit in Canada which have never been explored. I believe that young Canadians all over the Dominion if appealed to with courage, would respond to the national conception which inspired the fathers of Confederation; and I believe that there is not a province in Canada where the same attribute of simple courage—the rarest attribute of statesmanship, as John Morley used to say—would not command the same response that was so discernible in the old province of Quebec last October. That election, I am inclined to think, will one day rank as a turning-point in Canada towards better things. The Prime Minister (an interested observer to be sure) stated in a broadcast on October 31 that 'nothing which has happened in our country, since Confederation, has contributed more to Canadian unity'; and a French-Canadian cardinal, the highest dignitary of an historic church, speaking in Washington the other day, referred to the Quebec election as 'a vote for Canadian unity'. Provincial isolationism, like Canadian isolationism, is becoming obsolete. We must make the best living conditions we can with our fellow Canadians in this Dominion and with the best friends we can find in a rapidly contracting world.

IV

A third major factor in Canadian nationhood has passed through still greater vicissitudes during the last quarter of a century. The premature expansion of the Dominion to the Pacific in 1870-71 was followed by a cycle of railway construction and land settlement which was drawing very perceptibly to a close at the beginning of the last war. It was not finally liquidated, however, until 1930. In Canada as in the United States this cycle brought maladjustment and drastic problems of readjustment in its train. Old regional economies have broken down and new ones have been evolved. In one sense this growth has been the real stuff of nationhood. This 'great lubberly boy' for whom Elgin once predicted a rôle among the nations of the world has been growing up. He has been earning his own living and in all conscience he has taken on a man's job in this war.

The sixty-year cycle from 1870, when the Dominion undertook the administration of public lands in the West 'for the purposes of the Dominion' (in the words of the *Manitoba Act*), to 1930 when the remaining resources were given back to the Prairie Provinces, will always stand out in relief in the pattern of Canadian national growth. Much of this period was marked by frustration and disillusionment. The C.P.R. and a dozen 'colonization railways' were endowed with some

31,000,000 acres of western lands—almost exactly the area of England—all of it, as the railway land grants stipulated, 'fairly fit for settlement'. The utilization of this vast domain developed a number of unsuspected virtues in the railway land grant system, for the railway lands, restricted to the odd-numbered sections of the township, proved almost indispensable as reserves for the free-homesteaders on the even-numbered sections in developing the technique of summer-fallowing so necessary for successful dry farming on the Canadian prairies.[1]   The last of the railway land grants was made in 1894 but it was not until 1908 that the grants were all located and the whole system liquidated by the withdrawal of the railway reserves.

The opening of all remaining land reserves to free-homestead entry after 1908 raised the flood-gates for the settlement of semi-arid lands that ought to have been reserved permanently for the ranch or for irrigation.   The acreage under free homestead in Saskatchewan increased from 12,488,000 acres in 1906 to 29,000,000 in 1916.   In the three Prairie Provinces the free-homestead entries during the single decade from 1905 numbered more than 350,000—at 160 acres each, an area of more than 56,000,000 acres.   As late as 1918 railway lands and school lands and Hudson's Bay lands were still selling briskly under the stimulus of war prices for wheat, but the days of the free homestead were numbered.   The two major 'purposes of the Dominion' in retaining the public lands had been achieved, insofar as public lands could contribute to their achievement: as the Manitoba Resources

---

[1] The average farm in Saskatchewan is more than 350 acres of which only 160 acres could have come from the nucleus of a single free homestead.

Commission reported, 'the railways had been built and the lands settled'. When the remaining resources were transferred to the provinces in 1930 the other side of the medal came into view. After exhaustive soil and meteorological surveys by the Province of Saskatchewan it was found that more than one-tenth of the cultivated acreage of that province ought never to have been broken. From 1911 to 1931, 63,000 out of 110,000 homestead entries were eventually cancelled— about 57 per cent. Fifty-seven out of every hundred homesteaders never got across no-man's land to the point of owning their own homesteads. The great *Homestead Act* of the United States was once described as a wager in which the government staked a quarter-section of land that a man could not live on it for five years. In human material—the settler himself, his wife and family, the best years of their lives—to say nothing of farm buildings and equipment, the free homestead was a very costly expedient for the settlement of the frontier. Perhaps no government regulations could have withstood the mass migration which settled nearly a million people in the Prairie Provinces in ten years. The free-homestead system west of the hundredth meridian in the United States was still more devastating for the pioneer. As a matter of fact the federal administration of 'Dominion lands' from 1870 to 1930 challenges comparison with that of the United States at almost any point in the process. Some of the ablest men in Canadian public life administered the Department of the Interior. No finer record of trust in public lands is to be found in any country than the administration of school lands (sections 11 and 29 in each township) to produce

$67,550,000 in the school fund and current revenues up
to 1930 for the public schools of the Prairie Provinces.
At any rate the era of mass migration in North
America has now come to an end. There may be room
for one more 'swarm', so to speak, in the Peace River
district of Alberta, and readjustments on a prodigious
scale must yet be made. But for Canada as for the
United States a new cycle has begun, with readjustment and stabilization as the order of the day.
Professor Innis and Professor Bladen in the third and
fourth lectures of this series will speak with authority
on these and other trends in staple production and
population. But I think it will be conceded that the
economic and demographic basis of nationhood now
exists in Canada, and that the obligations in finance
and industry to be assumed by the Dominion in this
war are an imposing demonstration of national
maturity.

v

The fourth major attribute of Canadian nationhood
has come to maturity for the first time in our own day.
The functioning of Canada in international relations is
after all the symbol rather than the substance of
national growth. The apparel of nationhood is less
important than the maturity which makes that apparel
necessary and appropriate. The sartorial details which
are apt to obsess the adolescent mind are apt to
become commonplaces with adult responsibilities.
Young Canada may be a bit self-conscious in tails and
a white tie, so to speak, for the first time, but it is safe
to say that there is less of glamour than of grim
responsibility in a sense of youth and nationhood at

such a time as this. The threshold of another war is a sobering but appropriate place to measure these responsibilities, for beyond question international recognition was largely the result of deliberate policy at the close of the last war. 'The fact that the Oversea Nations (of the Commonwealth)', wrote Sir Robert Borden, 'had put into the fighting line larger forces than any but the principal powers probably decided the issue.'[1]

A share in trade and other treaties had long been a commonplace, of course, in Canada's external relations, under rigid direction and ratification by the Foreign Office of Great Britain. Sir Charles Tupper when High Commissioner had helped to negotiate trade treaties with Spain and France, and Sir Wilfrid Laurier after the French treaty of 1907 stated that 'the time has come when Canadian interests are entrusted to Canadians . . . A treaty has been concluded with France—a treaty which applies to Canada alone, which has been negotiated by Canadians alone.' A legation to Washington had been discussed as early as 1882 and again in 1892, but it was the war which swept these puny gestures into the stream of self-conscious nationhood.

As the war drew to a close the Canadian government developed very decided views upon the representation of the Dominions in the approaching Peace Conference and the projected League of Nations. Sir Alfred Zimmern, then serving in the Foreign Office, has left on record the consternation of the permanent officials when the Canadian views became known. Other nations could scarcely be expected to be more

---

[1] *Canada in the Commonwealth*, 1929, p. 96.

discerning. The path, Sir Robert Borden says, 'was at times rough and thorny', but 'in our advance along that path (he adds) the Dominion Ministers received from the British Prime Minister and his colleagues complete sympathy and unwavering support from first to last.' That seems to have been the story from beginning to end. The jurists and the pundits proved conclusively that the appropriate thing could not possibly be done, and then responsible statesmen proceeded to do it.

The British Empire delegation at the Peace Conference included five from the United Kingdom, seven from the Dominions and two from India. They ratified the famous memorandum of March 12, 1919, drafted by Sir Robert Borden and stipulating signature of the peace treaties and conventions by the Dominion plenipotentiaries. Paragraph 2 (of the memorandum) reaffirmed Resolution IX of the Imperial War Conference of 1917 that 'the organization of the Empire is to be based upon equality of nationhood'. The signature of the treaty itself was in the end anomalous, as Sir Robert Borden adds, for while the Dominion plenipotentiaries signed for the Dominions, the British plenipotentiaries signed also for 'the British Dominions beyond the Seas'. This anomaly was removed, as Sir Robert notes, by the procedure for treaties ratified by the Imperial Conference of 1926. In the League of Nations, for the first time perhaps, the nationhood of the Dominions 'was recognized (I am quoting from Sir Robert Borden's statement) as being in every respect equal to that of other members of the League'. The right of election to the Council of the League was vindicated only by a veritable mandamus signed by

Clemenceau, Woodrow Wilson and Lloyd George (May 6, 1919), and Canada was formally elected to the Council for 1927, the diamond jubilee of Confederation. Perhaps the greatest tug of war came with membership of the International Labour Organization in which the claims of the Dominions had to be carried to the Council of Four and pressed 'with the most resolute insistence'.[1] At the first International Labour Conference in Washington, 1919, Canada was formally elected a member of the governing body.

The establishment of Canadian legations in Washington, Tokio, Paris, Brussels, and also in the Dominions has been the work of scarcely more than a decade. Although discussed in 1882 a few years after the establishment of the High Commissionership in London, a legation in Washington was not authorized until the Paris Peace Conference[2] and was not actually established until 1927. The technique of treaties with foreign powers was finally formulated at the Imperial Conference of 1926—mutual consultation in matters of common interest and ratification by Dominion plenipotentiaries on the advice of Dominion ministers directly concerned.[3] The Canadian declaration of war on Sunday, September 10—just a week after the British declaration of September 3—was followed by the application to Canada by President Roosevelt of the *Neutrality Act* which had been applied to Great Britain during the previous week. Lord Balfour in a

[1] 'The Drafting Committee was peremptorily instructed to eliminate the objectionable clause and did so.'

[2] Announced on May 10, 1920.

[3] The Halibut Treaty of 1923 was negotiated by Canadians and signed by the Hon. Mr. Lapointe alone, but his appointment as plenipotentiary had still been made on the advice of British ministers.

moment of impatience with the intractability of foreign governments in recognizing the imponderables of the British Commonwealth, once exclaimed 'if International Law has not the sense to get over (these difficulties) we must manage as best we can.' Misunderstanding on the part of the United States, at least, would now seem to be a thing of the past. In any event Canadian nationhood, for many a day now, has been concerned with much more important issues, calculated to test these newly acquired responsibilities to the utmost.

VI

In one of the darkest hours of the civil war Abraham Lincoln once reaffirmed to a Canadian visitor— Alexander Tilloch Galt—his faith in the 'steady conduct of the American people'. The test of Canadian nationhood, after all, is our behaviour as a nation. A year or two ago the whole democratic world was passing through a period of low moral visibility. Even now (February, 1940) in this deceptive calm before the zero hour of the war, any thoughtful Canadian is apt to quail before the shape of responsibilities to come. It requires almost an effort to recall the contrasts of twenty-five years ago—the ingenuous response of 1914, the bands playing, the haste to reach the scene in time to share in the adventure. Canada was then a contributor (along with France, and Britain, and the Dominions, and Russia, and Belgium, and Portugal, and Italy, and Japan, and Roumania, and Serbia, and the United States) to a vast welter of world forces. In this war Canada is a senior partner, an arsenal for the Commonwealth and headquarters for the Commonwealth Air Training Plan which in combination with sea power may well have the casting vote in the war of material resources.

In the realm of the imponderables also, where alone victory can truly be won and consolidated, Canada can scarcely escape an unenviable responsibility. If ever there was a loathing for war in a man or in a nation it was surely to be found in the Prime Minister in the Dominion of Canada. 'Charged with the awful responsibility of prosecuting a war', Mr. King said at the beginning of this conflict, 'I have been compelled (contrary to every hope and wish I have ever entertained) to believe that only by the destruction of Naziism . . . can the nations of the British Commonwealth hope to continue to enjoy the liberties which are theirs under the British Crown, and the world itself be spared a descent into a new and terrible barbarism.' With this background of loathing for war, and the disintegration, in the sight of all men, of appeasement and every other desperate alternative to war, the only American nation as yet to sense this conflict in its real proportions may have a rôle to play, willy-nilly, in both hemispheres. Already, I am inclined to think, many of the distractions which imperilled Canadian national unity two years ago are appearing in their true perspective. Two years ago this continent could criticize with impunity. Today with a devastating clash of scientific armaments in prospect, with the outcome, in all probability, dependent upon civilian morale, in the last analysis perhaps the morale of women and children—of other men's women and children—there are not so many among us, like the high priest in the ritual of Leviticus, who can still stipulate a sacrifice without blemish and without spot.

Two years ago there were many on this side of the Atlantic who professed a duty to keep democracy pure and unspotted from the world. Today or tomorrow if freedom as we understand it is to pass under the cloud now gathering from the Rhine to the Volga—if the little free countries are to be blotted out, unaided, one by one, today, and the last of the big ones overwhelmed tomorrow—what would be the savour of our blessed democracy, I wonder, in our own nostrils, even on this continent? The gravest danger of Nazidom would come not by getting into this war but by staying out of it.

Believing as I do that some of us are still living in a fool's paradise in Canada, I cannot profess to see an untroubled prospect before Canadian nationhood, or before any other of our way of thinking. The prophets have had a bad time of it recently. I have noticed that the usual escape from one egregiously false prophecy, is to make two others which cannot possibly be falsified for ten or fifteen years. But whatever the remote future may hold for Canada, the national unity which has emerged from the chaos of two or three years ago is truly providential. It is worth reflecting that other great crises of our history have been marked by courage and statesmanship of a very high order. We may move from time to time in regions of low visibility, but I venture to conclude with the hope for Canadian nationhood which Edmund Burke expressed in vain for that lost world of an earlier day. 'Magnanimity in politics is not seldom the truest wisdom. . . . We ought to auspicate all our public proceedings in America with the old warning of the Church, *Sursum corda!* Lift up your hearts. We ought to elevate our minds to the greatness of that trust.'

II. FEDERAL RELATIONS IN CANADA SINCE 1914

by D. G. CREIGHTON

I

IT has often been pointed out that federalism represents a compromise between the forces which are making for unity and nationalism and those which are making for regionalism and diversity. In a federal state, whose citizens really desire union without unity, the centre of political pre-eminence will tend inevitably to shift and oscillate. In one period the federal authority may acquire a position of leadership which in another era it will be obliged to surrender in whole or in part to the province or states. These changes in relative position are determined largely by social forces in the broadest sense of the term—by geographic, economic, cultural, political and military factors; but these factors, it should also be remembered, must operate in and through a body of constitutional rules. It is true that these rules, under the pressure of human demands and requirements, may be changed; they may be changed either by formal legislative amendment or—what is often equally effective—by judicial interpretation. But in Canada these agencies of change either do not exist or remain relatively unsusceptible to the influence of native Canadian forces. The absence of any recognized and accepted method of formally amending the *British North America Act,* in important particulars, has served to place in the hands of the Judicial Committee of the Privy Council the vast responsibility of adapting the Canadian constitution to the tasks of a changing world. The Judicial Committee, which is, of course, completely external to Canada, has proved itself singularly inflexible in the maintenance of its principles. In other words, the rules count always in a federal system; but they perhaps count particularly in Canada.

It is therefore of importance to know something of the substance of these rules as they stood in 1914. A student desirous of discovering the guiding principles of modern Canadian federalism will look in vain for many of them in the Resolutions of the Quebec and London Conferences. It might almost be said that he will look in vain for many of them in the plain terms of the *British North America Act.* People continue to study the deliberations of the Quebec and London Conferences under the impression that they are actually investigating the abiding principles of the Canadian federal system; but, on the constitutional side at least, such historical exercises have long ago ceased to have much more than an antiquarian interest. It is not in the Resolutions accepted at Quebec, but in the decisions rendered by the Judicial Committee of the Privy Council that we may discover the nature of modern Canadian federalism. The Fathers of Confederation may have framed the *British North America Act;* but it is the stepfathers of Confederation who have moulded the present Canadian constitution.

To the vast majority of Canadians the very existence of the Judicial Committee of the Privy Council is probably unknown or only dimly suspected. Even to the informed minority it remains an abstraction of which the distinguishing feature is an awful finality. It is like an omnipotent impersonal force, a divinity so dread that we cannot even invest it with anthropomorphic characteristics. The aspect which it bears for the whole empire has nowhere been better indicated than in an anecdote told by Lord Haldane, who himself became one of the leading figures in the Committee in the twentieth century. A traveller, so runs Haldane's story, had penetrated into a remote part of India and there found a native tribe which was engaged in the pious exercise of offering sacrifices to a remote but all-powerful God. The traveller inquired the name of this divinity. "We know nothing of him", was the reply, "but that he is a good god and that his name is the Judicial Committee of the Privy Council."[1] This was a reply which evidently moved Lord Haldane profoundly; and there can be little doubt that he consoled himself with the reflection that the poor Indians did but represent the reverent and unquestioning faith of the entire empire. And, so far as Canada is concerned, there is a good deal of evidence that Lord Haldane was quite right.

When, however, we try to improve upon the knowledge of the Indians without impairing the reverence which we share with them, we discover that information concerning the Judicial Committee is extremely hard to come by. In the absence of learned treatises, we cannot do better than turn to the occasional articles which Lord Haldane himself has written on the body of which he was so distinguished

---

[1] R. B. Haldane, *Education and Empire, Addresses on Certain Topics of the Day* (London, 1902), pp. 124-5.

a member. These articles acquaint us informally with the great importance and endless variety of the business of the Committee. It works, as Lord Haldane is never tired of telling us, for a vast part of the empire; it finally determines the affairs of an endless variety of peoples according to the legal principles appropriate to each. "We sit there", said Lord Haldane, "to administer Buddhist Law, or Hindu law, or Mohammedan law, one after the other. We administer Roman-Dutch law from South Africa or from Ceylon, or French law from Quebec, or the common law of England from Ontario, or curious mixtures of law which prevail in various colonies, sometimes Italian law, sometimes Roman."[1] An expert knowledge of one of these legal systems might be regarded as a respectable accomplishment for an ordinary man. But the titans of the Judicial Committee, from long practice and profound study, have grown accustomed to the multifarious and exacting requirements of their office; and they apparently leap, with the agility of quick-change performers, from one legal metamorphosis to another. "My Lords", said Lord Haldane on one occasion, when he was still a barrister pleading before the Committee and not a member of it, "I am addressing your Lordships, not as seven English Judges who require to have foreign law proved to them, but as seven Cadis of the Mohammedan religion who are presumed to know the Koran."[2] The seven Cadis, who appear momentarily to have forgotten their parts, responded to the call of the prompter and Lord Halsbury

[1] Haldane of Cloan, "The Work for the Empire of the Judicial Committee of the Privy Council" (*Cambridge Law Journal*, vol. I, pp. 143-55).

[2] *Ibid.*, p. 152.

searched his well-worn Koran on the spot. To an outsider it might seem that there was at least the faint possibility of some bewilderment and confusion in these endlessly varied deliberations. The outsider might even be so far misled as to conceive of a noble judge who continued obstinately to peruse the Koran when he ought to have been consulting the *British North America Act*.

Of all the judges who sat in the Judicial Committee of the Privy Council during the nineteenth century, William, Lord Watson, was perhaps the most important from the point of view of the Canadian constitution. He was a Scotsman, who received his first important appointment from Disraeli. According to his ardent admirer and pupil, Lord Haldane, he came down to London "knowing nothing"; but apparently, by assiduous reading of the Koran, he managed to correct this somewhat serious deficiency. He was a man of admirable independence of mind. On occasions he would invite Haldane to his chambers to talk over a point of a case in which Haldane was not concerned. The consultation, according to Haldane, apparently consisted of this—that Lord Watson would recite the arguments on both sides and would then declare that he thought the conclusion perfectly clear. "What he wanted", writes Lord Haldane most disarmingly, "was an audience."[1] Indeed, Lord Watson appears to have been quite impartial in the matter of audiences. Sometimes the audience was Haldane in Lord Watson's chambers, and sometimes the audience was the lawyers of the Dominion of Canada in Lord Watson's court; and perhaps the second contributed

[1] *Ibid.*, p. 150.

about as much as the first to the elucidation of Lord
Watson's mind. Lord Watson's mind, in fact, pursued
its objective in admirable independence of mere external influences. To uninitiated Canadians the terms
of the *British North America Act* have even today
an odd look of simple clarity; but to Lord Watson,
who worked with all the advantages of a knowledge
of the Koran, of the Roman-Dutch law of Ceylon
and of the jurisprudence of the Channel Islands,
there appeared mysterious beauties in the statute
which were hidden from the more limited vision of
colonials. The constitution, as Lord Watson left it,
may have been better or worse than that which the
Fathers of Confederation intended; but it is difficult
to argue that it was not materially different. Lord
Haldane, indeed, considers the Canadian constitution
to be one of the principal monuments to Lord Watson's
personal fame. "In a series of masterly judgments",
wrote Haldane, "he (Lord Watson) expounded and
established the real constitution of Canada."[1]

The *British North America Act of 1867* grants to
the provinces sixteen exclusive powers of a local
character. It confides to the Dominion the exclusive
residuary power of a general character; and, for
greater certainty but not so as to restrict the general-
ity of the grant, it declares that this residuary authority extends to twenty-nine powers which are then
enumerated as examples of the general right to legislate for the peace, order and good government of
Canada. Under the decisions of the Judicial Committees, the general direction of which may be said

---

[1] Quoted in F. R. Scott, "The Royal Commission on Dominion-Provincial
Relations" (*University of Toronto Quarterly*, vol. 7, Jan. 1938, pp. 141-51).

to have been supplied by Lord Watson, these principles have been developed into the constitution as we know it today. The residuary power of the Dominion has been almost completely divorced from the enumerated powers and Lord Watson actually went so far as to declare that it was supplementary to them. The enumerated powers have, in effect, become the normal legislative powers of the Dominion; the general residuary authority has become an ambiguous power which has validity almost solely in times of crisis; and thus the examples have virtually swallowed up the principle which they were intended to illustrate but not to restrict. The legislative competition between the Dominion and the provinces has thus been brought down to a conflict between the enumerated powers of each. While certain of the Dominion's enumerated powers have been divested of any real authority, the provincial power to legislate in relation to property and civil rights in the province has been given an extended scope; and there is some truth in the charge that it has become the real residuary clause of the Canadian constitution.

These two powers—the residuary authority of the Dominion to legislate for the peace, order and good government of Canada and the authority of the provinces to legislate in relation to property and civil rights, are the two powers which will concern us most in this paper. Long ago, before it had come under the influence of Lord Watson, the Judicial Committee, in awarding an early decision to the Dominion, had declared that "few, if any laws, could be made by Parliament for the peace and order and good government of Canada which did not in some incidental way affect property and civil rights."[1] The so-called Prohibition case of 1896, in which the judgment was delivered by Lord Watson, decided that in normal circumstances national legislation which incidentally affected property and civil rights was legislation which trenched upon property and civil rights and was therefore *ultra vires* of the Dominion. The Dominion was thus on the way to losing the vast field of authority which had been indicated by the Judicial Committee in its early opinion; and the residuary authority of the federal legislature was coming to be regarded as an overriding power which could be exercised only in cases of national emergency. This, roughly, was the position in 1914.

II

The coming of the war profoundly altered the relationship between the Dominion and the provinces which had been established during the previous decades. It did this for several reasons. In the first place, it aroused political, economic and social forces in Canada which demanded and required Dominion leadership; and, in the second place, it constituted an obvious national emergency which permitted the Dominion to escape temporarily from the restrictions which the Judicial Committee had imposed. Canada entered the war unanimously, as one people; the war, as it progressed, involved the whole of Canada as one people; and these facts furnished the solid foundations of Dominion predominance. The conflict, which was

[1] *Report pursuant to Resolution of the Senate to the Honourable the Speaker by the Parliamentary Counsel, relating to the Enactment of the British North America Act*, 1867. . . . (Ottawa, 1939), Annex 3, p. 17.

by far the greatest political effort in which Canada had ever been engaged, aroused a national patriotism which found its inevitable focus in the Dominion. The tasks of the war, which laid the whole economy and the entire population under conribution, required a centralized control which only the Dominion could supply. The Dominion, in short, possessed both the moral authority and the natural right to lead the nation; and it became the controlling and directing agency of all effort to achieve that common purpose which, in the early days of the war, did so much to unify the Canadian people.

It was decided, moreover, that the Dominion, by virtue of its power to legislate for the peace, order and good government of Canada, could exercise the controlling authority which the situation appeared to demand. Back in 1896, in his decision on the Prohibition case, Lord Watson had admitted that matters which were in their nature local and provincial might, in certain circumstances, attain such dimensions as to affect the body politic of the Dominion as a whole and thus to justify federal legislation. The war now supplied a definition, if not a complete definition, of what these exceptional circumstances were. Under the *War Measures Act,* which was passed in the emergency summer session of 1914, the Dominion began to take a number of steps which it would never have dreamed of taking in times of peace; and these were subsequently validated by the Judicial Committee on the basis solely of the crisis which the conflict had created. Thus the Dominion may be said to have acquired two federal constitutions: one for affairs in Canada and the other for wars in Europe.

The emergency constitution would no doubt be invoked for a war in North America; but so far we have happily not experienced such a conflict. The emergency constitution could almost certainly not be invoked for any other probable catastrophe on this continent, for in the last ten years we would appear to have experienced almost every conceivable kind of crisis and, until September 1939, the emergency constitution has never for a moment been restored. Thus on the basis of the facts of our experience we can provisionally conclude that a crisis is truly Canadian only when its centre is physically outside Canada. This may be said to have been Lord Haldane's great contribution to the Canadian constitution.

Armed with these unprecedented constitutional powers and strong in the moral support of an aroused people, the federal government plunged into the new national policy of war. It assumed enormous burdens; but in order to sustain them and to reach its objectives, it extended its activities, multiplied its controls and regulations and vastly increased its demands of the Canadian people. Little by little, as the war became more total in character, the Dominion was driven to the attempt to order and direct the entire life of the nation toward the one supreme purpose. The greatly enlarged sphere of its activities came to embrace fields of state control which no government in Canada had ever entered before and which, in ordinary circumstances, could only be regarded as provincial in character. Federal boards were established to direct the production, conservation and sale of foodstuffs, to regulate the distribution of fuel and to fix the prices and control the marketing of wheat. The War Trade Board, which was perhaps the supreme manifestation of the controlled wartime economy, was, in February 1918, granted sweeping powers "to carry out such supervision as may be considered necessary of all industrial and commercial enterprises in Canada." These unusual economic controls were accompanied by unprecedented financial requirements. The Dominion, which had never before imposed direct taxation, established the Income and War Profits taxes. It pursued inflationary policies which assisted in the creation of huge funds available for investment; and it then proceeded to float war loans to the amount of hundreds of millions in the Dominion, whereas before the war not five million of federal bonds had ever been disposed of in Canada. More and more, the efforts, sacrifices and enterprises of a whole people were dominated by a single purpose and regulated according to a single pattern, which the Dominion designed and controlled. The provinces, which tried merely to assist in an effort whose direction they never aspired to share, were reduced to a position of relative unimportance. In the main, they did not renew their demands, financial and otherwise, upon the Dominion. The Dominion did not exercise its traditional controls, such as disallowance of provincial statutes, upon the provinces. And, for a short time at least, the discordant sounds of sectional disputes and Dominion-Provincial disagreements died almost completely away. The Dominion stood at the zenith. Its predominance was unquestioned, and, in the first years of the war, it appeared almost indefinitely assured.

III

Yet, as it turned out, there was something quite deceptive about these appearances. The relative position of the Dominion and the provinces began once more to alter; and before long, the federal government was being displaced from the unaccustomed eminence to which it had been temporarily uplifted. In part this new reversal of fortunes was the result of general movements in the early twentieth century in which the war was merely an incident of major importance. But, in part also, it was the direct result of the war; and the signs of its coming began to multiply long before the war was ended.

The first thing to go was the moral solidarity of the nation upon which the wartime predominance of the Dominion was so largely based. This is not a particularly pleasant subject to recall; but it is an essential part of the story; and if we dismiss it unhistorically from our minds, we may be quite sure that other groups in Canada will not. On the whole, the Canadian people were practically unanimous about the wisdom and necessity of the end for which the war was being fought; but they could not be persuaded to agree indefinitely about the means by which Canada should attempt to reach the accepted objective. In part this disagreement was the result of the character of the war and in part the consequence of the diversified composition of the Canadian people. The war did not bring with it an invasion of the Canadian homeland or a direct menace of an attack upon its frontiers; and the absence of this simplest and most irrefutable of all necessities for union, permitted variations of opinion concerning the extent and character

of the part which Canada ought to play in the
conflict. The diversity of Canadian life—in terms of
races, occupations, interests and loyalties—began once
more to manifest itself. From the very beginning of
the war, there had been differences in the response
of Canadians to the conflict; with the formation
of the Union Government and the inauguration of
conscription in 1917, these differences became open
and acute. Resistance to conscription, which was
certainly most determined and violent in Quebec,
was by no means confined to that province. Throughout the Dominion, Trades and Labour Councils pro-
tested against conscription. It was accepted by the
farmers of Ontario only on the express condition that
liberal exemptions would be granted to agricultural
workers; and when, in the spring of 1918, these
exemptions were cancelled, thousands of angry farmers
descended upon Ottawa to voice their protest to the
Union Government. During the election of 1917,
which sustained the Union Government, racial passion
in Canada reached a new climax of bitterness; and
in January, 1918, the Quebec legislature actually
debated a resolution which envisaged the secession
of the province from the Union.

Thus the military demands of the war created the
first divisions in the wartime unity of the Dominion.
These divisions were deepened and multiplied by the
economic costs and social burdens of the conflict
which were distributed unequally among the Canadian
people. In order to assist the financing of the war,
the federal government pursued inflationary measures
which served to raise the cost of living steeply. The
inflation brought good fortune to those who profited

from war industries and from rising land values, but it brought little but trouble to most skilled tradesmen and white-collar workers, whose real wages perceptibly declined. The protest against the human sacrifices which the war had involved was now followed by the clamour against the classes which the war was supposed to have benefited and against the economic system whose inequalities the war appeared to have made more glaring and oppressive. Before the war, Canada had believed itself to be a land of equality of opportunity; but the war increased the social stratification of the country and deepened the class consciousness of its component groups. From 1917 to 1922, the economic distress and social unsettlement which was common to the whole of western society was reflected in class and sectional protests throughout the Dominion. The formation of the One Big Union in the west, the Winnipeg strike, the establishment of Farmer's Governments in Ontario and Alberta and the election of sixty-five Progressives to the Dominion House in 1921 are striking manifestations of this protest movement. The old-line parties, the Liberals and Conservatives, had claimed that they had successfully reconciled the various group interests of the community in a common national interest. But now this national interest was attacked as inequitable, and the parties which professed it were put upon the defensive. The collapse of the Liberal party during the war was now followed by the collapse of the Union Government; and for a while it seemed as if the old basis of national politics was visibly disintegrating.

This decline of national solidarity along political and social lines was accompanied and followed by a loosening of the economic ties which bound the various parts of the Dominion together. In Canada, the growth of national unity is dependent, to a large extent, upon the successful integration of the various regions of the transcontinental economy; and this integration is ultimately based upon the paramountcy of the east-west transport system which has been built upon the St. Lawrence and the transcontinental railways. During the war and much more ominously in the 1920's, the east-west route began to decline as a unifying factor in Canadian economic life. The bankruptcy of the Grand Trunk Pacific and the Canadian Northern Railway suggests the increasing weakness of the old national system, while the opening of the Panama Canal and the development of provincial highways illustrate the growth of new transport routes which were chiefly of regional significance and which undermined the supremacy of the old east-west scheme. The frontier in the west, which had been the property and concern of the whole nation, declined in relative importance. There arose a series of northern regional frontiers, which became the monopolies of the different provinces concerned. The central provinces and British Columbia prospered in the early 1920's, while the Maritimes and the west were still depressed; and it seemed for a while as if the country was disintegrating into a disconnected succession of regional booms and regional depressions. The successes and failures of regionalism both served to undermine faith in the economic nationalism of the past; for while the failures were incurred in despite of the national system, the successes were achieved in partial independence of it.

There can be little doubt that the weakening of these economic, social and political bases of nationalism served in the early 1920's to undermine the position which the Dominion had occupied during the war. There were, however, still other factors in the situation. The Dominion seemed to have lost some of the bases of national support; but it also appeared to be reaching the embarrassing position of having attained its principal objectives. It had built the transcontinental railways, created a national industry and settled the west. Through the establishment of full Dominion status it was about to gain the form of political nationhood most acceptable to the Canadian people, and, through participation in the war, it had already acquired a measure of international recognition. These, indeed, were formidable achievements; but is there not, in the very word "achievements", a certain ominous ring of finality? Were not the tasks which the Dominion had essayed appropriate chiefly to the early, the formative period of nation-building? And did not their successful completion itself imply that Canada had now moved on to a more mature and complex stage of its history in which the old Dominion functions would count for less and less? How far was the federal government able or willing to assume the tasks appropriate to maturity? The war had brought the conception of the social-service state to Canada. The Dominion had organized for war; why, said the protest groups, should it not now organize for economic welfare and social security? In this programme of the future, what part was the Dominion likely to play?

The Dominion, sad to relate, found itself both inhibited and prohibited from action. It was held back, in the first place, by the very magnitude of the burdens it had accepted during the war. From 1913 to 1921, the national debt increased sevenfold— from half a billion to three and a half billion; and of this vast increase, the major part was accounted for by war expenditures, for which, of course, there were no productive assets at all. In the same period, from 1913 to 1921, the current annual expenditure had increased roughly threefold—to about $350 million; and of this sum nearly half was expended to service the war debt and to discharge other current obligations which the conflict had created. In other words, the Dominion was obliged to perform a function which was totally new in its history: it was required, every year, to transfer vast sums of money which added nothing whatever to the sum total of public services which it performed for the community as a whole. It took from the people in general the money which was required to pay pensions and to discharge the interest on war loan bonds, of which about four-fifths were in the hands of large corporations and wealthy individuals. Thus the very classes which had suffered most from the inflation were now required to pay an inequitable portion of the cost of the war; and, on the other hand, they obtained little or no compensation from the Dominion in the shape of enlarged government services. Under such cautious financiers as Mr. Fielding and Mr. Robb, the post-war federal governments abandoned all thought of new and expensive projects and sought merely by the strictest economy to reduce controllable expenditures and to balance the budget. Once again, the Dominion was obviously more preoccupied with the burdens of the past than with the problems of the future.

The federal government, however, was not only deterred by its own inhibitions: it faced positive prohibitions as well. As soon as the years of crisis were over, the peace-time constitution was re-established; and the Dominion found all about it the forbidding restrictions of property and civil rights. It was at least arguable that the problems of industry, labour and social welfare had become really national in scope during the course of the war; but no argument was possible, in terms of Canadian values, for the Judicial Committee of the Privy Council simply reimposed the old prohibition which prevented the Dominion from passing any national legislation whatever, in virtue of the peace, order and good government clause, which even indirectly and incidentally affected property and civil rights. In 1922, the *Board of Commerce Act* was declared *ultra vires* of the Dominion and in 1925 the *Industrial Disputes Act* suffered the same fate. The Dominion, in short, had been ejected from a large part of the field of social and economic legislation; and it proceeded to retire almost completely, heaving, it may be suggested, a great sigh of relief.

The very factors which tended to decrease the importance of the Dominion served also to enhance the consequence of the provinces. As the centralizing influence of the national transcontinental system declined, provincial or regional economies emerged with greater clarity; and while the functions of the federal government remained relatively stationary, the responsibilities of the provinces increased in number and gravity. During the 1920's, they incurred heavy capital expenditures for provincial public works and development schemes—for hydro-electric commissions, highways, railways, public telephones, irrigation schemes and colonization projects. They improved protective services for labour, developed health services and assumed a number of social obligations which in the past had been borne by relations, neighbours or private charities. Inevitably, the interest of the populace became focussed upon the provinces in much the same way as it had been upon the Dominion in time of war. As Prime Minister Taschereau said proudly at the Dominion-Provincial Conference of 1927, the provinces were "closer to the people". The political power of the provinces, and their conscious-ness of political power, steadily increased during this period. The 1920's was a great era for the ventilation of provincial rights. Ontario reaffirmed the Compact Theory of Confederation—the theory, that is, that any change in the *British North America Act* requires the unanimous consent of the provinces. The west contributed the doctrine that the beneficial control of natural resources is historically and constitutionally vested in the province—a doctrine which meant that the Dominion, having assumed control of the lands of the western provinces, should now restore what remained of them with compensation. The Mari-times, on their part, presented the thesis of Maritime Rights, in which it was asserted that the Atlantic provinces had been induced to enter Confederation on the strength of certain representations and promises, which had never been fulfilled and must now be carried out. Broadly speaking, the Dominion surrendered its position in all these matters.

There remained, however, certain great and obvious weaknesses in provincialism. The provinces were assuming vast and increasing responsibilities, which the

Fathers of Confederation had never expected or intended them to assume, and for which they had made no adequate financial provision at all. There were, moreover, profound differences between the provinces in respect of their geographic advantages, natural resources and economic development; and these variations were, and are, naturally reflected in the revenue and credit power of the different provincial administrations. The provinces, in short, had made commitments and accepted tasks which all of them would find difficult to sustain in times of depression and which some of them found hard to carry even in times of prosperity. The Dominions with its vast credit and unlimited taxing powers, might have supported these burdens more easily, despite the load left by the war; and through the extension of its own federal services, it might have effected the transfers between richer and poorer regions which seem necessary to maintain common standards throughout the country. But, as we have seen, the Dominion was prevented from increasing its services, in the direction in which increases were most needed, by the constitutional rules. It could, of course, assist the provinces by giving them unconditional subsidies or grants in aid. Payments to the provinces were, as a matter of fact, increased during the late 1920's, at the instance of the Maritimes and the west; and by 1930, the Dominion was paying out annually about $17 million in unconditional subsidies. The existing system of subsidies, in both theory and practice, is, however, open to the gravest objections; and it may be said that it has never solved the problems of weak regions and depressed areas, even when the regular payments have been supplemented, as during the depression, by enormous emergency transfers. Thus, in the late 1920's, the situation was full of danger. A serious gap had already appeared between the resources and the obligations of Canadian governments. The Dominion, with potentially far greater tax and credit power, had, for one reason or another, been obliged to adopt a negative and cautious attitude. The provinces, with weaker resources, had accepted commitments and responsibilities the pressure of which threatened to become unendurable.

IV

At this point, the depression descended upon Canada. It was a national calamity of the first order. But there were variations in adversity as in prosperity; and it was the export, staple-producing regions of the country which were particularly hard hit. A succession of crop failures, due to drought, soil-drifting, grass-hoppers and rust, combined with unprecedented low prices for farm products, brought the west, and particularly Saskatchewan, to its knees. Under the blows of the depression, the existing division of functions and revenues between the Dominion, the provinces and the municipalities simply collapsed.

Whatever the governments of Canada tried to do, the ineffectuality of the existing arrangements was evident. Even if they had confined themselves to mere palliatives, the breakdown of the constitution was still inescapable. Sooner or later all governments suffered loss of revenue and confronted new and rapidly rising expenditures; but, inevitably, this combination of financial evils was most acute for those regions and those governments upon whom the burden of relief measures chiefly fell. Though the municipalities and provinces had never, of course, experienced anything comparable to the distress occasioned by the depression, the obligation to provide relief for unemployment, was historically and constitutionally theirs; and, to a greater or lesser extent, they were incapable of performing those social functions whose constitutional control they clung to with such determination. The Dominion was obliged to step in. In the first place, it assumed part of the burden of relief, according to proportions which were occasionally revised, and, in certain particularly distressed areas, such as in Saskatchewan, it paid the total cost. In the second place, it came to the rescue of the financial solvency of certain western governments, who were unable to meet ordinary expenditure, even with Dominion aid for direct relief, and who rapidly came to the end of their tax and credit powers. It must be emphasized that these were purely exceptional and emergency payments, for which there was no provision whatever in the existing financial arrangements of the constitution. In depressed regions, therefore, and particularly in Saskatchewan, provincial responsible government and all the community services which it provided, were in large measure sustained—and even then inadequately—by these enormous transfers from the Dominion.

When, however, the governments of Canada tried to turn from palliatives to more positive measures, then the weaknesses and limitations of the constitution became still more conspicuous. For some little time, of course, governments showed little tendency to depart from the accepted policies of the past. The federal

Conservative administration, for example, which had been elected largely on its claim to end unemployment, was inclined at first to follow methods—such as raising the tariff—which were mostly quite orthodox in their conservatism and certainly quite unexceptionable in their constitutionality. Whatever beneficial effect these policies may have had was felt more in the central than in the other provinces; and, therefore, early federal measures did little to minimize the economic and social differences between the provinces which the depression tended to increase. The drift towards regionalism, which had begun in the decade following the war, became still more pronounced. In the absence of a new national policy which might have served to lift the country collectively out of its apathy and distress, the provinces naturally followed the first law of self-preservation; and the new provincial governments, which assumed power in the early 1930's after a series of electoral "landslides", began to identify themselves ever more closely and exclusively with the dominant economic and social interests peculiar to their own areas. With few exceptions, each of these new governments embarked upon a provincial recovery scheme, designed to remedy the troubles most characteristic of the region and to satisfy its distinctive grievances. In popular estimation, Prime Minister Aberhart was the outstanding example of this; but Messrs. Macdonald, Duplessis, Hepburn and Pattullo all illustrate, to a greater or lesser extent, the same general tendency.

There were, and are, however, obvious limitations to the effectiveness of any purely provincial scheme, as Mr. Aberhart and others have discovered. As bad times continued, a confused demand arose for a positive national attack upon the depression and also upon the "system" which was popularly supposed to have caused it. The Co-operative Commonwealth Federation, founded in 1932, gave vigorous expression to this demand and significantly adopted a national approach to the whole problem. Undoubtedly, however, what chiefly lent popularity and prestige to the idea of a national plan was the election of President Roosevelt in the United States and the inauguration of the National Recovery Administration in 1933. Everybody was suddenly talking about planning; and the Liberal and Conservative summer schools, held in 1933, gave evidence that the old parties were already disposed to reshape and restate policy in response to the new economic and social demands. In February, 1934, Prime Minister Bennett moved for the appoint-ment of a committee to investigate price spreads and the effect of mass buying.

As soon, however, as the Dominion government approached the question of reform legislation, it immediately confronted the limitations of property and civil rights. The Prime Minister began to argue in favour of constitutional amendment; and, during 1934, he made a vain attempt to reach an agreement with the provinces in the matter of revisions. When these efforts failed, he decided upon a direct and much more radical approach. In January, 1935, in a series of five radio addresses, he announced a programme of reform legislation, which, with amendments, was passed in the subsequent session of the federal house. The merits or demerits of the Bennett "New Deal" need not detain us here; but obviously the "New Deal" was of great historical importance, for it constituted both a comprehensive approach to the problems of the new, post-war Canada and a frontal attack upon the limitations of the constitution. As hardly needs to be mentioned, the attempt failed. It was politically defeated in the Canadian general election in 1935 and it was legally annihilated by the Judicial Committee of the Privy Council in 1937. The *Minimum Wages Act*, the *Limitation of Hours of Work Act*, the *Weekly Rest in Industrial Undertakings Act*, the *Unemployment and Social Insurance Act* and the *Natural Products Marketing Act* were all declared to be *ultra vires* of the Dominion. Thus the work which had been so ably begun by Lord Watson and so efficiently continued by Lord Haldane, now reached its final completion. The Dominion was constitutionally incapable of legislating in respect of a domestic national crisis; and the provinces, by their individual efforts, were likely to find it difficult, if not impossible, to achieve a satisfactory collective result. The constitution had at last reached the impasse towards which the forces of the war and post-war periods had been progressively driving it.

Mr. Bennett's methods had completely failed; and Mr. King was not disposed to continue them. In 1937 a Royal Commission on Dominion-Provincial Relations was appointed to investigate the original settlement of Confederation in the light of the economic and social changes of the past seventy-five years, and to suggest means by which a more satisfactory balance of functions and revenues might be achieved. The original members of the Commission were the Honourable N. W. Rowell, Chief Justice of Ontario (Chairman), the

Honourable Thibaudeau Rinfret, a Justice of the
Supreme Court of Canada, Dr. J. W. Dafoe, of the
Winnipeg Free Press, Dr. R. A. MacKay, of Dalhousie
University, and Professor H. F. Angus, of the Univer-
sity of British Columbia. Unfortunately, Mr. Justice
Rinfret was compelled to resign from the Commission
very early in the proceedings on account of illness; and
Chief Justice Rowell, after having taken an active
part in the work during the first eight months, was
regrettably forced to retire for the same reason. Dr.
Joseph Sirois, of Laval University, took Mr. Justice
Rinfret's place; and, when Chief Justice Rowell's
resignation was reluctantly accepted by the government, he succeeded to the position of chairman. It
appeared at first as if all the provincial governments
would co-operate in the work of the Commission; but
subsequently the government of Alberta declined to
participate; and, in Quebec, counsel representing the
province declared to the Commissioners "that we are
not appearing before your Commission either as an
applicant, nor as a defendant, and that we shall not
feel bound, in any way whatsoever, by the opinions
contained in your report."[1]   The government of
Ontario presented a brief to the Commission and at
first participated fairly fully in its work; but, in July,
1938, it declined to co-operate further, alleging that the
Dominion had committed a virtual breach of faith in
altering the incidence of the Income Tax before the
Report of the Commission had been received. In spite
of these rebuffs and in spite of the casualties in its own
personnel, the Commission persevered successfully

[1] *Report of the Royal Commission on Dominion-Provincial Relations,*
Book I, p. 16.

in its attempt to complete a comprehensive and detailed examination of the entire problem. It held sittings in the capitals of all the provinces, recorded over ten thousand mimeographed pages of evidence, and filed 427 exhibits from recognized public organizations, including, of course, the provinces themselves. Moreover, it instituted an elaborate programme of independent research which was carried on contemporaneously with the public hearings and which included a comparative study of the public finances of all the provinces and the Dominion for the past twenty-five years. Finally, in May 1940, the Commissioners' *Report,* which, including the numerous appendices, totalled over thirty volumes, was presented to the Dominion government.

In the long run, the *Report* will certainly be regarded as one of the greatest state papers in the entire history of the British Empire. It includes both a comprehensive, factual survey of the problem of Canadian federalism in its historical development, and a constructive balanced programme of reform. In effect, the Commissioners have proposed a systematic re-allocation of government functions and revenues which will enable the country as a whole to meet the need of economic control and social welfare which has grown so rapidly with the coming of national maturity. The Dominion, according to the plan, will assume the burden of provincial debt, together with the most costly of all the social services, unemployment relief; but, in compensation, the federal government is to be given the exclusive right to levy the progressive taxes by which these services can be most efficiently borne. The provinces are to be required to surrender the existing unconditional subsidies, as well as the income, corporation and inheritance taxes; but, on the other hand, they will be enabled, through the proposed system of National Adjustment Grants, to maintain the residual social and developmental services at the average Canadian standard without exceeding the average Canadian rate of taxation. Jurisdiction in the contentious and difficult fields of labour, marketing and insurance has been re-allocated between the Dominion and the provinces with due respect for that basic distinction between "national" and "local" interests which served the Quebec Conference so well; and the thoroughgoing nature of the proposed redistribution can better be appreciated when it is realized that, under the proposed new system, the whole—or nearly the whole—of the "New Deal" programme of 1935 would probably be regarded as constitutional by the courts.

The new Fathers of Confederation have performed a creative act comparable to that of the Quebec Conference and in harmony with its guiding principles. For the moment, the crisis of the war has inevitably distracted public attention from their proposals; but, in all probability, the conflict will increase, rather than diminish, the need for reorganization; and it is to be hoped that the entire *Report,* as a related whole, will receive the most serious consideration in the not too distant future and that positive action will result. It is to be hoped also that the proposed revisions will not be judged exclusively from the point-of-view of either Dominion or provinces, but will be considered broadly from the standpoint of the Canadian system in its entirety. Dominion and provinces, after all, are simply two systems designed to serve the needs of the Canadian people; and the claims of either one of them to represent a political principle of superior sanctity and virtue should be regarded with detachment. We have a right to require the efficient and harmonious co-operation of the partners in our federal system, for we have needed it in the past and we shall need it in the future. We are at present engaged in a war for the defence of democracy and international justice. Nothing is more likely than that the future will confront us with a domestic struggle for the maintenance of values which we cherish deeply. Canada is a country with certain undeniable weaknesses, which, as recent events have shown, may become terribly acute. It is possible that we may have to fight—and fight hard—for the preservation of the institutions and standards of living which we believe to be our rightful heritage. And one of the main conditions of success is the reform of a federal system which, at least in some vital respects, has become antiquated, unbalanced and inequitable.

III. ECONOMIC TRENDS

by H. A. INNIS

THE attempt to control and direct our own destinies since we emerged from the intense baptism of fire of the last war has been evident in every phase of economic life. The growth of nationalistic determinism has not been peculiar to Canada but has reflected a general trend of the war and post-war period throughout the world. The war speeded up the prosperity which began with the turn of the century, following the long period of depression from 1846, and which ended with the severe crisis of 1929. Those who believe in the regularity of cyclical activity describe a long wave from 1896 to 1933, a shorter wave from 1922 to 1933 and a very short wave from 1929 to 1933. All of these coincided to produce the unprecedented severity of the latter year. Those who are concerned with a more detailed description of cyclical activity regard the long depression as one characterized by extensive construction of railroads or as industrial capitalism with dependence on coal, and the long period of prosperity as one characterized by new sources of power such as gasoline and electricity or as marked by the entrenchment of metropolitanism and the growth of finance capitalism. The crisis and the depression exposed the limitations of finance capitalism and were followed by the spread of national capitalism.

The sources of the material for this paper reflect perhaps more effectively than any other index the growth of nationalism. One may point to the amazing growth of the Dominion Bureau of Statistics under Dr. Coats who assumed direction in 1918, registered in an ever widening range of census material, an ever increasing stream of publications, and an ever expanding size and weight of the *Canada Year Book*. Provincial governments have followed—two of them, strikingly enough at the extremities of the Dominion, having established economic councils. Universities have increased the size of departments concerned with the social sciences. The revival of the Canadian Political Science Association was followed by the publication of the *Canadian Journal of Economics and Political Science*. The *Canadian Historical Review*, developed into a quarterly immediately after the war. American foundations have supported Canadian scholarship in facilitating the research and the publication of the results in volumes in the Canadian Frontiers of Settlement series and the Canadian-American Relations series. The man on the street has been persistently educated in the patter of economics by the daily press and the development of a more efficient specialized press in such media as the *Financial Post*. Large scale production of paper, the extension of printing presses, and the development of the aeroplane and the radio have speeded up communication and made it possible for electorates to be swayed by the new gospels of social credit, poverty in the midst of plenty, production for use and not for profit, and all the rest.

The character and extent of economic literature have been profoundly affected by secular and cyclical activity. It is not the point of this paper to present an economic interpretation of economic bibliography, but the decline of immigration, the disappearance of free land and the onset of the depression have brought a wide range of problems which are reflected in the reports of the commissioner of the *Combines Investigation Act,* of the Tariff Board, and of Royal Commissions on regional problems particularly in the Maritimes and the prairies, on banking, railways, price spreads, and on special industries such as wheat, coal, and textiles. These documents have the smell of political bias, the evidence presented to the bodies concerned reeks with the claims of special interests, and the debates about them are designed to catch every conceivable political breeze. Provincial governments have made extensive inventories of their resources and supported directly and indirectly numerous royal commissions and investigations.

The voice of the economist is heard throughout the land. In every investigation economists of quality and quantity have contributed substantially either by giving evidence or by stuffing the shirts of their betters, i.e. writing the final reports. The rise of economists has been an important political trend of the post-war period. They have captured crucial positions in the civil service especially with the Bank of Canada, and the discussion of the problems of Canadian recovery has taken on the air of rational calculation. Every large organization concerned with business has its economist. A new religion has emerged. The acute religious controversies of the past generation have given way to economics. One would like to believe that the continuous and rapid growth was important to the extension of knowledge.

> But men at whiles are sober
> And think by fits and starts. (HOUSMAN)

All of this is presented by way of credentials and to show that I am aware of the relatively slight but important rôle which economics has to play. While we have established the new priesthood to which every venture must in some way pay tribute, our religion is sufficiently young to permit of disputation, and I may be permitted for this reason to point to some trends which may not be in every way conceded.

> They answered as they took their fees
> There is no cure for this disease. (BELLOC)

I

The last war hastened a trend of rapid exploitation which began early in the century and slowed down in 1929. A brief description of the major developments in separate regions will indicate more clearly the place of various industries. The stimulus of the cyclonic economic activities of the Pacific in the early part of the century to transcontinental traffic and industrial development in eastern Canada began to show striking signs of decline. The centre of the spectacular outburst in the Yukon had declined to the point in 1926 where empty houses were conspicuous and the only evidences of activity were the operations of a few large dredges systematically exploiting the remaining placer gold of the large rivers and the small scale operations of individuals and partnerships on the creeks. The engine which had run on the short railway of the district in the height of its prosperity stood in its stall with little prospect of being moved until the crack of doom. A tourist trade attracted by the log cabin in which Robert Service formerly lived brought money into a region which formerly produced it. Fur farming and shipments of concentrated ore from the silver lead camp at Mayo emerged from a scene of desolation and wreckage. Church and state retreated on all fronts. That pioneer of missionary effort in the Arctic and the Yukon, Bishop Stringer, was leaving to become Archbishop of Rupert's Land with his headquarters at Winnipeg. A community which thought only of dollars as the smallest units had gradually become reconciled to quarters and finally to dimes. The high price of gold during the depression and the low price of commodities brought a revival, but the pulse beat was feeble.

Completion of four railways from the prairies to the coast of British Columbia immediately before the war, two by the Yellowhead Pass and one each by the Kicking Horse and the Crowsnest Pass, three to Vancouver and one to Prince Rupert, unlocked the resources of the province. Fresh halibut was sent by express from Prince Rupert to the markets of eastern Canada and the United States. Canadians and Americans pushed to more distant fishing grounds of the Pacific and eventually reached the point when exhaustion compelled the adoption of mutually restricted operations in the Halibut Treaty of 1923—significantly enough the first to be signed by Canada with the United States without the intervention of Great Britain. The salmon fishery of the Fraser River was subject to the same trends toward depletion and a later convention between Canada and the United States pointed to the need of a mutual policy of conservation.

The lumber industry after the turn of the century flourished in relation to local demands, to the demands of an expanding market in the prairies and to the demands of Pacific regions, especially the Orient. Completion of the Panama Canal immediately after the war opened the industrial regions of the Atlantic to the lumber producers of the Pacific. Lumber pushed its way into the markets of eastern Canada and responded to the housing boom in England. Cheap water navigation extended the range of markets for a heavy bulky commodity and the new industrialism based on oil and hydro-electric power lowered costs of transportation and created markets on the Pacific and the Atlantic. Similar rapid expansion of the pulp and paper industry assumed expansion of hydro-electric power. Ships were attracted to British Columbia ports for enormous quantities of raw materials, including wheat from Alberta, and they brought in ballast manufactured products which penetrated far to the interior.

As in the Yukon the mining boom of the Kootenay area in the late nineties suffered a temporary collapse but interest shifted from the precious metals to the more permanent development of base metals. In the war period copper deposits were exhausted and intensive experiments solved the problem of handling complex Sullivan ores and led to the enormous investment of capital in hydro-electric power, concentrators, refineries and fertilizer plants at Trail. Coal mines in the Crowsnest Pass area and Vancouver

Island suffered from the competition of hydro-electric power, and oil from the Pacific States. Specialized agriculture responded to the demands of the prairies, the urban population of British Columbia, and the markets accessible by the Panama Canal. Irrigated fruit farming of the Okanagan and dairy production of the Fraser valley were faced with intensive competition on the export markets, and there emerged a demand for systems of control and, in the case of fruit, exposure to inquiries and prosecutions under the *Combines Investigation Act*.

Exhaustion of resources, the increasing importance of large scale capital equipment and the attractions of a pleasant climate to labour from the prairie regions led to demands for restriction of Oriental immigration and to the enactment of legislation barring both Chinese and Japanese. Oriental labour was driven by regulations from the mines, the lumber camps and the fishing industry and took refuge in agriculture and commercial activities. We shall leave the Pacific Coast conscious of an intensely specialized economy developed at great cost in the face of topographical restrictions but expanding under the stimulus of new sources of power and the advantages of enormous improvements of navigation. Depletion of resources, exposure to the effects of fluctuations in the prairie markets and competition in the export markets have contributed to the demands for controls and to the difficulties of controls. A marked concentration of population about Vancouver and Victoria facilitates the organization of local demands.

In the vast area east of the Rocky Mountains and west of Fort William and north from the 49th parallel to the Arctic we have suggested the effects of expansion on the Pacific in the shipment of wheat from Alberta and of products from the Pacific coast to the interior. Settlement was extended to the Peace River and wheat was grown in larger quantities. The high prices of the war and the sharp decline after the war were followed by gradual improvement under the influence of speculative activity in North America prior to recovery in the wheat producing regions of Europe. Construction of branch lines, the efficiency of new sources of power in tractor, truck, and combine, the introduction of new varieties and the expansion of the pooling system facilitated concentration on wheat. Collapse of the boom in 1929, low prices of wheat and years of drought converted an area of high purchasing power to one marked by emigration, drastically reduced standards of living, relief, and debt with serious repercussions for railways, industry and finance. The tragedy of the wheat producing areas was offset in part by a shift to dairying and livestock and was accompanied by phenomenal expansion in the vast area dominated by the Canadian shield. In 1924 the Peace River, the Slave, and the Mackenzie Rivers flowed serenely to the north with only the disturbance of the ordinary routine of the summer season. The Hudson's Bay Company had just completed another amalgamation with its rival the Lamson Hubbard Company after the difficulties of fabulous prices of fur during the war and the disastrous collapse which followed. Fur trading posts had been extended among the Eskimo along the Western Arctic following up the Canadian Arctic expedition in the search for supplies of white fox. More efficient transportation had been introduced. Imperial

Oil had discovered petroleum at Fort Norman, but it was not developed until the discovery of radium ore on Bear Lake created new demands.

The Panama Canal not only lowered costs to the Pacific and Northern Alberta but it also hastened the development of the mineral resources of coal and oil in southern Alberta. Moreover it hastened the development of trade to Bering Sea and around the north of Alaska. Its effects in opening the north were reinforced by a further major development of transportation, the Hudson Bay Railway. The discovery of a successful flow sheet by Mining Corporation led to the development of Flin Flon and Sherritt Gordon by the Hudson Bay Mining and Smelting Company and to construction of branch lines of railway, a smelting plant, and a hydro-electric power plant on the Churchill River. Experience gained in constructing the railway to Flin Flon led to the rapid construction of the Hudson Bay Railway to Churchill in the winter season of 1928-9. The Hon. Frank Oliver, who had long cherished the dream of the West for an outlet by Hudson Bay, was one of the first to visit the new port in 1929. The firm of James Richardson sent the first small consignment of wheat via the Hudson Bay route in the same year. Completion of the railway was followed immediately by prospecting activities by air from points along the west coast of Hudson Bay, the Western Arctic and the Mackenzie. Many will remember the dangerous adventure of Col. McAlpine in the fall of that year. The extensive prospecting investigations were followed by discovery of the mineral wealth of Bear Lake and of Slave Lake. The Mackenzie River became a centre of intensive prospecting and mining for minerals and oil and contributed materially to make Canada the most important country in the world in the handling of freight by air. The fur trade was extended to the extreme eastern part of the Arctic at King William Land and on the island of Somerset. Final evidence was collected on the tragedy of the Franklin expedition. The Hudson's Bay Company established contact with the last band of Eskimos and completed an activity which began with the first landing of Europeans on the shores of temperate North America, and finally completed the northwest passage as a commercial route. Governmental activity was in evidence in scientific investigations and conservation. Depletion of animal life led to steps which involved the heroic and successful undertaking of driving a reindeer herd from Alaska to the Mackenzie delta.

The movement of the economic height of land eastward from the Pacific Coast in which the influence of the Panama Canal penetrated far into the interior and encroached on the sphere of the St. Lawrence meant intensification of industry along the Atlantic seaboard at the expense of industry in the heart of the continent, and had implications direct and indirect for eastern Canada, particularly in the depression. Enlargement of the Welland Canal, improvement of the Erie Canal and improvement of harbours in Canada and the United States in part offset the effects of the pull of the Pacific coast but the St. Lawrence canals have still to be deepened. Through the Panama Canal came butter from New Zealand to harass the Canadian dairy industry and to lead to the demand for, and the introduction of, protective tariffs. Lumber from the Pacific coast was sold in the markets of eastern Canada in

competition with the local product. Fruit from British
Columbia came into competition with fruit from eastern
Canada. Railway expansion in the prairie regions no
longer created demands for rails and equipment from
the steel mills and car plants of Ontario, Quebec, and
Nova Scotia. Decline in demand for steel meant
decline in the demand for Nova Scotia coal. Companies
were reorganized, and subventions were paid to increase
the market for coal in Ontario.

The Canadian lumber industry had long felt the
effects of demand from the increasingly urbanized
markets of the United States. Control of land, timber,
minerals, and power sites by Ontario enabled her to
engage in reprisals against tariffs imposed by the
United States by embargoes on logs and pulpwood cut
on Crown lands. Ontario attempted to compel American capital to establish plants in Canada, but with
exports permitted from private lands and without an
embargo in Quebec and New Brunswick, was only
partially successful. Depletion of American supplies
of pulpwood, the demand of American newspapers for
cheaper raw material and the imposition of an embargo
in Quebec in 1910 and in New Brunswick a year later
were followed by a lowering of the tariff on newsprint
in the Reciprocity Treaty of 1911 and a further
lowering in 1913. The way was prepared for migration
of the industry to Canada. The demand for newsprint
during the war and the cutting off of supplies of
sulphite pulp from Scandinavia were followed by a
sharp rise in prices. The investment of large profits
from war undertakings in advertising rather than in
payment of profit taxes supported a continuation of
high prices but ultimate readjustments brought a dras-

tic decline. Bankrupt sulphite plants came on the market as a result of renewed Scandinavian competition. The necessity of lower costs hastened the construction of large plants such as that of the International Paper Company at Three Rivers. Newsprint mills were closed down in the United States and the power sold to industries and municipalities. Power sites were acquired in Canada to support the newsprint industry and ultimately, as in the United States, municipalities and industries. The Duke fortune from tobacco was invested in the Duke Price power and paper developments on the Saguenay. On the Ottawa, the St. Maurice and the Saguenay and even on the rivers of the Hudson Bay drainage basin made accessible by the National Transcontinental, forests of spruce and balsam, cheap navigation, power sites, labour conditions, and a short rail haul to New York and the Atlantic seaboard combined to encourage numerous and enormous undertakings. The upward swing of the business cycle gathered momentum, and brought increased demands for advertising space and for newsprint, and a widespread familiarity with bonds, arising from the war, made funds available for construction. The crisis of 1929, the depression, and the development of new methods of communication in the radio were followed by low prices, disaster, reorganization, and the end of the period of colossal undertakings. Paper companies became increasingly concerned with power with the result that it tended to become the main product and newsprint the by-product. The difficulties of Abitibi in the development of power plants and the advantages to newsprint mills on the Ottawa of power contracts with the Ontario Hydro-

Electric have been centres of intense political interest
in Ontario. With high prices during the last war large
numbers of newspapers like the *News* and the *World* in
Toronto disappeared and with the difficulties of the
depression the *Globe* and *Mail* were amalgamated.
Partisanship becomes less conspicuous as the traditional dichotomy of the Liberal and Conservative
press disappears. Advertising returns from department
stores become a more important source of revenue.
The significance of the radio has been evident on all
sides. We have witnessed a revolution in the technique
of communication far more significant in its implication
than the change from the movies to the talkies or the
vogue of Charlie McCarthy.

A discussion of the problems of newsprint and
hydro-electric power is drawn irresistibly into a discussion of another major industry which has depended on
power development, namely, mining. The *Globe and
Mail* has been supported by capital from mines. As in
British Columbia mines have been opened, exploited,
and exhausted, but the industry has shown greater
evidence of continuity and expansion. The enormous
nickel deposits at Sudbury were rapidly exploited
during the last war and a refinery was built at Port
Colborne. The end of the war, naval limitation
agreements, and the demand for lighter battleships
with the use of new sources of power such as oil, compelled the industry to concentrate on the discovery of
new uses. New alloys were worked out and industry
was provided with more efficient raw materials. A
world monopoly was strengthened in the amalgamation
of the International Nickel and Mond in the late years
of the twenties. Cobalt emerged as a great poor man's

silver camp early in the century but its properties were exhausted by capitalistic devices in the war and the post-war period. We know of the wealth which poured from this region through the benefactions of the late Col. Leonard, of the O'Briens, and others. Companies transferred their activities from Cobalt to Porcupine and began the development of such gigantic properties as Dome, McIntyre, and Hollinger. We know of the generosity of the Dunlaps. From the rich mines of Kirkland Lake we have had Dr. J. B. Tyrrell, Mr. Wright of the *Globe and Mail,* and Sir Harry Oakes. Capital from Hollinger contributed to the construction of the smelter at Noranda. As companies accumulated surpluses, and mines were exhausted, there came the search for other properties with the success we have described in Flin Flon in northern Manitoba and the development of properties in northern Quebec. Nipissing, Mining Corporation, Dome, Hollinger, and the others have ceaselessly examined possible developments in the whole of the vast Pre-cambrian area. Moreover a widespread interest in penny stocks, the financial interests of Toronto, Buffalo, and New York, independent financiers, brokers, and governments have been responsible for large numbers of developments such as those in the Patricia district and elsewhere associated for example with the name of Mr. Hammell. Hydro-electric power has kept pace. Power released from exhausted mining camps, such as Cobalt, power developed with the newsprint industry, power supported by private enterprise and governments directly and indirectly concerned with mining met the demands of the industry. Island Falls, Abitibi, Quinze and numerous other sites have emerged. The effects of the

demands of expanding industries in mining, pulp and
paper, and hydro-electric power have been evident in
the growth of a more highly integrated industrial
region in eastern Canada shown in the establishment
of the Ontario Research Foundation and the National
Research Council. A divergence of interest has grown
up within Canada—the prairies with wheat dependent
on Great Britain, the East with less dependence on the
prairies and with greater dependence on new industrial
products for the markets of the United States.

The pull of the densely populated areas of the
eastern States has been evident not only in the regions
tributary to the St. Lawrence but also in the Maritimes.
After the last war mine sweepers were converted into
trawlers and the production of dried cod was enormously increased in Iceland. This increase in production
pushed cod from Newfoundland out of European
markets to the markets of the West Indies and South
America. In turn Nova Scotia was unable to compete
with Newfoundland and she sought protection in the
sheltered market of the St. Lawrence region and in the
United States. She was compelled to turn from the
dried fish industry to the fresh fish industry. Salt gave
way to ice. Refrigeration and rapid transportation
involved capital equipment in the form of trawlers,
freezing plants, and fish meal plants. The American
market became more important with exhaustion of
resources, increased population, and speeding up of
transportation. The live lobster trade extended from
western to eastern Nova Scotia and the Magdalen
Islands. American capital became dominant in the
Maritime fresh fish industry in the late twenties.
Retreat from European to North American markets

imposed tremendous strains on the Atlantic industry. These were evident in the greatest of all tragedies for democratic populations—the disappearance of responsible government in Newfoundland and in St. Pierre and Miquelon. In the Canadian Maritimes direct and indirect subsidies, and a healthy interest in their own problems as shown in the active co-operative movement have relieved the starkest aspects. All around the shores of Nova Scotia, New Brunswick, Gaspé, the Canadian Labrador, Newfoundland, and the Newfoundland Labrador, disturbances in the economic life in the countries bordering the Atlantic were felt directly and immediately. War in Spain, the imposition of sanctions on Italy, the collapse of the coffee market in Brazil, the problems of sugar in the West Indies—each of these was registered in the price of cod. Nova Scotia apples were faced with competition from British Columbia. New Brunswick and Nova Scotia became concerned with the pulp and paper industry as a result of competition from the Pacific. Iron and coal suffered from higher costs of production and the decline of markets for rails in the prairie regions.

Throughout Canada but particularly in the more densely populated regions of the east adjacent to the United States petroleum as a new source of power became the basis of an enormous programme of road construction on the part of the provinces. The construction industry, the automobile industry and a host of subsidiary industries flourished. The tourist trade was encouraged by favourable exchange rates, and we capitalized on the "noble experiment" by repealing prohibition. The fishing fleets converted their schooners into rum runners. Encouragement in the use of new sources of power by the province increased the difficulties of the railroads dependent on coal and in turn of the Canadian Pacific Railway and the federal government.

To summarize, the last war intensified the demand for fur, fish, wheat and other food products, newsprint and minerals. In the post-war period lowering of costs of transportation through the use of the Panama Canal and the use of oil in travel by air, water, road, and railroad brought an extension of production in the vastly extended area tributary to the Pacific coast. It became possible to travel to Moosonee and to Churchill by pullman and to cover the vast areas of the Mackenzie and the Yukon by plane. We have seen these developments, most of us, in our own time. Cheaper products from the Pacific coast hastened the growth of industries and the concentration of population along the Atlantic seaboard. New sources of power and the significance of technological change in transportation to the movement of cheap bulky commodities such as timber and of light valuable manufactured products implied profound disturbances to the industries of North America. The framework of the industrial structure of the pre-war period was subjected to terrific bombardment by a revolution affecting heavy staple products. Economists have paid insufficient attention to the specific effects of these changes on specific commodities and specific industries. In Canada as in the United States population began to move eastward rather than westward. The quota imposed by the United States hastened urbanization of population and a decline in the birth rate. It was significant that the Anglo-Saxon population ceased to have a majority in Canada. I shall not discuss the implications of declining birth rate in European populations to problems of labour, trade, and strategy during the present war. We must be content to point to the increasing importance of the markets of the United States to Eastern Canada as a result of increasing population and exhaustion of resources.

II

The United States in the pre-war period was a debtor nation; in the post-war period a creditor nation. With large supplies of gold, a population trained in the use of securities as a result of war finance, a powerful financial centre in New York, and an agricultural and industrial plant fresh from the war effort, she was reluctant to face the effects of competition from the imports which characterized a creditor position. High import tariffs and enormous loans enabled her to increase exports and to participate in the task of European reconstruction. To a large extent loans were made by which reparations were paid by Germany to pay the Allied debts to the United States. Moreover, the disappearance of debts in Germany through the drastic effects of inflation enabled cities and towns and industrial plants to secure new mortgages for extensive renovations and improvements. The Versailles Treaty prohibited the draining of funds into armaments and led to concentration on commercial aviation, and development of the electrical, chemical, lignite and iron and steel industries. Germany purchased Wabana iron in Newfoundland in competition with Nova Scotia.

The intense speculative boom in the late twenties in the United States, supported by the technological advances we have described, and evident in the loans for Canadian pulp and paper plants, roads, hydro-electric power plants, and skyscrapers of the cities of North and South America, began to reverse the process and to drain funds from Europe. Wheat, newsprint, minerals, commodities and securities, governments, private traders and wheat pools were carried along in the upward sweep. The effects of the crash in 1929 and the depression which followed spread rapidly throughout the entire world. The collapse of specu-lative markets was marked by the sharp fall in prices of securities and commodities. Governmental credit felt the effects. The long series of attempts to reinstate Austria after the vast empire of 1914 had been dismembered and carved into separate states centring about Prague and Budapest eventually faced defeat. The bankruptcy of one of the largest banks in Vienna in May, 1931, and attempts to check disaster forced one country after another off the gold standard and finally England was pushed into the arms of a National Government in September. The Ottawa Agreements of 1932 and the election of President Roosevelt were a part of the attempts at recovery in the British Empire and the United States. The banking crisis in the United States in 1933 was followed by the ill-fated World Economic Conference.

The significance of the refusal of the United States to participate effectively in the World Economic Conference warrants careful study. The long period of the wars of the last half of the eighteenth and the early nineteenth centuries in some sense solved the problems of commercial capitalism since the American revolution was followed inevitably by the trend toward free trade in Great Britain, and by the second Empire.

But it was precisely the contributions of the United States to the solution of the problems of commercial capitalism which made it impossible for her to solve the problems of finance capitalism. Active governmental intervention in a European war involved enormous loans to the Allies, a strong creditor position, and marked technological advance. High tariffs and private loans to enable Europe to repay the interest on government loans contributed to the impasse of 1929 and 1933. The United States following the traditions of commercial capitalism repelled political entanglements in Europe but the war and finance capitalism brought entanglements of a more subtle character. Nevertheless President Roosevelt continued the policy of his predecessors and where loans had been made to finance exports he raised the price of gold to $35 an ounce in order to compel other countries to sell that commodity in return for American dollars with which they could purchase American goods.

The effects of this policy varied widely. With the end of the period of reconstruction in Europe, nations imposed tariffs on wheat and other commodities partly on grounds of retaliation against the United States and partly in the interests of self-sufficiency for military purposes and to check the drain of gold. Russia with the assistance of European and American engineers and five-year plans had reached the point where she became a competitor in European markets. Gold bloc countries were forced off the gold standard. Finally attempts were made to re-establish certainty in exchange by the development of exchange equalization funds and the introduction of the Tripartite agreement between France, England, and the United States in

1936 and the addition of other countries at a later date.

The immediate effects on Canada became evident in marked activity in gold mining and in base metal mining where gold was a by-product. The pulp and paper industry gradually recovered from the low point of the depression. The indirect effects were more difficult to trace. The long series of devices of the United States to maintain a relatively rigid continental price structure had its effects on the more elastic price structure of maritime areas. The last war weakened the dependence of the Orient on Europe and hastened the industrialization of Japan. The disastrous effects of the fall in prices in 1920 on the silk industry were followed by the earthquake of 1923 and the financial panic of 1927. In spite of these difficulties Japanese textiles began to extend their markets in the far east and India was compelled to raise her tariffs. Lancashire was severely affected and began to press for a share of the markets of Canada and the other Dominions. Wheat and wool moved in large quantities from Australia to Japan. The depression was accompanied by determined efforts to extend markets in China by conquest.

The Antipodes were closely tied to the price structure of Great Britain and reflected its difficulties. Great Britain had suffered from attempts to catch up with the gold standard in the twenties. A temporary boom in coal mining, following occupation of the Ruhr by the French in 1923, was marked by higher prices, and the difficulties after its evacuation were followed by the general strike of 1926. With the crash in the United States and the drastic fall in prices of raw materials Great Britain was at last in a position to gain. The light industries had expanded rapidly in the south with the difficulties of the heavy industries in the north. A housing boom created demands for British Columbia lumber. The dominant position of Washington and Oregon in the world's lumber market was lost and British Columbia took their place. There was a dramatic reversal of positions as a result of the price lifting policies of the United States and the higher costs. While the lumber industry flourished, the dairy industry felt the effects of competition from the Antipodes and took refuge behind tariffs and the creation of boards designed to support the fluid milk industry, and to increase the consumption of that product. There were attempts to gain access to the American market. Low prices of grain favoured a shift to the production of bacon for export to Europe.

It is picturesque to describe the United States as an island of dollars floating in a sea of sterling but it is not accurate. It was rather a centre of disturbance in the wide sea of the world's economy sending out currents affecting at various points the centres of Canadian life depending on whether they produced minerals, especially gold, and newsprint, or wheat and lumber. To widen the channels of influence of the American price lifting policy and to narrow the discrepancy between American and world prices the Hull treaties were designed to provide a series of sluiceways or an anchorage for the American economy. These sluiceways enabled Canadian products to penetrate the American market at certain points.

The discrepancies between sterling and the dollar introduced innumerable strains between the areas affected in Canada, and compelled a resort to various expedients. We adopted a wheat board and guaranteed a minimum price for wheat. We defaulted on debts and introduced various adjustment schemes. Railway rate legislation improved the position of the extremities of the Dominion, the Maritimes, and British Columbia. The Bank of Canada emerged to cope with the problems arising from our dependence on staple products for export to Great Britain and the United States. The old provinces with control over their own mineral and pulpwood resources felt immediately the effects of the New Deal and were more advantageously situated than the new wheat producing provinces with more direct dependence on Great Britain. To investigate these problems it was necessary to appoint the Rowell Commission.

Adjustments between Canada and the United States have involved not only the introduction of internal machinery. Specially designed arrangements such as the Halibut treaty and the Salmon treaty were concerned with conservation. The International Joint Commission, among other tasks, made extensive investigations leading to the proposals for deepening the St. Lawrence waterway. But the problem of reaching agreements was complicated by the character of the constitutional framework. Constitutions designed for defence are not adaptable to co-operation. The Senate of the United States is a notorious stumbling block to treaties. It is paralleled by the position of the old provinces in the Confederation of Canada. Nationalism is entrenched in constitutional handicaps. The extent of its influence has been evident in the difficulties of co-operation between labour organizations of the United States and Canada.

Strict avoidance of political activities has facilitated affiliation between the Trades and Labor Congress and the American Federation of Labor and the relatively rigid relationships between railway wages in Canada and the United States, but it has not prevented the isolation of the unionism of the French Canadians and the unpleasantness over the C.I.O.

Rigidities in some relationships between Canada and the United States have accentuated concentration on flexibilities in others. Labour is largely restricted from migrating to the United States but the tourist trade is an object of intense interest on the part of Canada. Capital movements have been encouraged in every possible way. American firms have not only responded to encouragement but have been quick to see the implications of differences in price levels or of instability in American policy and have set up branch plants to take advantage not only of the Canadian market but also of the diverse markets provided by Imperial and other agreements. The automobile and the agricultural implement industries will serve as illustrations. The aluminum industry on the Saguenay was a result not only of the search for investment in hydro-electric power development by the Duke interests but also of the search for a means by which the Aluminum Company of America can participate effectively in a world cartel. American industry has recognized the importance of maintaining a position in other countries to offset the effects of disturbances in the United States. Properties are bought in Canada to hedge against inflation in the United States. The state prohibits us from owning gold, but we can still buy gold stocks and gold mines. The state has resorted to control over gold as a means to security and has made insecurity more inevitable.

Economic trends, or perhaps we should say political trends, in Canada have been and will be powerfully influenced by political trends in the United States. These are primarily concerned with internal problems and it would be dangerous to predict as to their solution. National finance capitalism in other countries has followed the path of direct governmental control of exchanges and of the direction of economic and political energies to military ends concerned with immediate or ultimate conquest or resistance to conquest. Colonies have become important as a means of expenditure to support policies of full employment and not as a direct means to wealth. They have come to serve as economic balance wheels. Ethiopia could scarcely be regarded as an asset under any other circumstances. Colonies as a means of expenditure have not been thought of by the United States although the vacillating policy toward the Philippines might be regarded as partaking of that character. The same could not be said of military and naval expenditures including bonuses to veterans. The interest in less tangible forms of conquest such as spheres of influence in South American republics and in China may become more important. Canada in her own interests as well as in those of the United States should be constantly alert to the implications of American policy. In a world in which nations and particularly the United States concentrate on their own problems and the use of the new machinery of the modern state, Canada is in a very dangerous position. European civilization has moved from an emphasis on land under feudalism, to an emphasis on trade under commercialism, to an emphasis on money under finance capitalism. We have not yet solved the problem of working with gold or working without it. The democratic countries have gone so far as to co-operate in agreements and the struggle at the moment is between co-operation and coercion. Those words of Lewis Carroll assume ominous import.

> He thought he saw a banker's clerk
> Descending from a bus,
> He looked again and saw it was
> A hippopotamus.
> "If this should stay to dine" he said
> "There won't be much for us."

It may seem preposterous that Canada should entertain the alternative of coercion but there is all too much evidence that the dangers to which we have been exposed have led us to follow precedents created elsewhere and to establish new ones. Compulsion has reared its ugly head where co-operation was the password. In British Columbia in the fruit industry and in the dairy industry supreme court decisions have been invalidated by legislation compelling numbers outside the co-operatives to abide by the decision of the majority. In the prairie provinces compulsory legislation has found its way on the statute books. Even in the federal field the *Natural Products Marketing Act* was prevented by a privy council decision. In the west and the east, boards have emerged with a powerful element of compulsion. One expects manufacturers to follow merchants who in the words of Adam Smith are 'silent with regard to the pernicious effects of their own gains. They complain only of those of other people.' 'People of the same trade seldom meet together, even for merriment and diversion, but the conversation ends in a conspiracy against the public, or in some contrivance to raise prices. It is impossible indeed to prevent such meetings by any law which either could be executed or would be consistent with liberty and justice. But though the law cannot hinder people of the same trade from sometimes assembling together, it ought to do nothing to facilitate such assemblies; much less to render them necessary.' The commissioner of the *Combines Investigation Act* regards all this as a normal course but he does not consider political compulsion. Nationalism is still the last refuge of scoundrels. There are well meaning leaders of large organized religious bodies who argue for toleration and compulsion in the same breath. The dangers of national finance capitalism have been acute in Canada. With the construction of boards and the complicated machinery which has emerged in Ottawa since the war the dangers are not less, and considering the inexperience of those who man such recently installed devices, are much more.

> Oh! let us never never doubt
> What nobody is sure about. (BELLOC)

Nor is the British Empire a final bulwark. With scarcely a word of dissent responsible government was dismissed in Newfoundland as a constitutional nicety by a Royal Commission presided over by a labour peer. Good government is no substitute for self-government.

At the moment we are concerned with the immediate world problem of resisting coercion by force of arms. It is a second effort and the more important for that. It is essentially a part of the inevitable tradition of Canadian life—one would hope—of neither accepting nor imposing domination. Only in such a world could we of all countries have lived and only in such a world can we live. It may seem strange that the United States should have blazed the way to this freedom and that we should be compelled to participate in a struggle to maintain it. But it is more vital to us than to her since she has grown into other ways.

> And how am I to face the odds
> Of man's bedevilment and God's?
> I a stranger and afraid
> In a world I never made. (HOUSMAN)

IV. POPULATION PROBLEMS AND POLICIES

by V. W. BLADEN

AS a basis for discussion of problems and policies it is necessary to devote the first part of this lecture to an outline of the trends of population growth in the last two centuries. To many the facts to be cited will be familiar, for the last two or three years has seen a flood of books and magazine articles on various aspects of declining population.[1] But the importance of public education in this matter seems amply to justify the repetition of familiar facts. I shall therefore examine in some detail the history of population growth in England and Wales, and the present prospects for its further growth. I shall then deal more briefly with other European countries and with the United States. The second part will deal with some of the problems which confront Europe and the United States as a result of the approach of an era of stationary, or declining, population. In the third and final part, I shall be concerned with the probable effects on Canadian population and prosperity of these momentous changes in Europe and the United States.

[1] See V. W. Bladen, "The Population Problem," *Canadian Journal of Economics and Political Science*, November 1939.

I

We know very little about the size of the population of England before 1700. The first census was not taken till 1801, and civil registration of births and deaths was not introduced till 1837. Such evidence as we have, however, suggests that, though there may have been fluctuation, there had been no marked trend of growth or decline for several centuries. In the eighteenth century an era of population growth began, and after 1770 the rate of growth was rapid. The immediate cause of this growth was a decline in mortality resulting from progress in medicine and public health. As a result of this "medical revolution" the mean expectation of life rose from about 30 years in 1750 to 40 years by 1850. The improvement in infant mortality and in maternal mortality was particularly striking. This improved mortality meant a decrease in the death rate from over 30 per thousand in 1750 to 20 per thousand in 1820. With the birth rate relatively stationary at a high level (something over 30 per thousand) this fall in the death rate produced a sharp rise in the rate of natural increase, and a consequent rapid growth in population. The coincident revolutions in agriculture and industry were necessary conditions for this growth, not, as is rather generally supposed, the immediate causes. Without them the "devastating torrent of babies", which the new medicine enabled to survive infancy, could not have been fed, clothed, and housed; the "positive checks" of Malthus would have come into play; the death rate would have risen as poverty triumphed over medical science. In time, perhaps, the slow operation of those processes of social adjustment, about which we know too little, might have reduced the birth rate to a level consistent with the low mortality and the limited productivity. For the fifty years, 1770 to 1820, the increase in productivity resulting from the application of science to agriculture and industry did take care of the increase in population resulting from the application of science to medicine and sanitation. The fact that the death rate rose a little after 1820 suggests that the growth of population then became too rapid, that population pressure did develop, and that the positive checks did operate. A perusal of the report of the royal commission on the health of towns (1844) suggests an alternative explanation of this check to the fall in the death rate: the new demands on the sanitary engineer were heavy and the lack of adequate institutions of local government hampered him in meeting these demands.

After 1870 mortality again improved. The mean expectation of life, which was a little over 40 years in 1870, had risen to over 60 years by 1933. The death rate had fallen from 22 per thousand to 12 per thousand over the same period. But in this period the birth rate, which had remained more or less unchanged throughout the eighteenth century and the early part of the nineteenth century, at over 30 per thousand, began to fall. By 1933 it had fallen to 14 per thousand. Thus the excess of births over deaths, the natural increase, which had been 13 per thousand around 1870, had fallen to 2 per thousand by 1933. Acceleration in that decline of fertility which began about 1870, and retardation of the continuing decline in mortality, seems to be bringing the modern era of population growth to a close. Indeed the end of that era is closer than one might suppose from the figures so far presented. A study of the changing age composition of population would show that it is becoming less favourable for births and more favourable for deaths as the proportion of older people is increasing. The present small excess of births is likely, therefore, to become a deficiency in the near future. The present fertility of the population is insufficient to maintain its numbers, and, though some further improvement in mortality may be expected, this is not likely to be sufficient to offset the effect of low (and probably still declining) fertility.

Dr. Kuczynski has rendered notable service to demography, and particularly to public education in demography, by introducing a simple measure of the degree to which populations are replacing themselves, known as the "net reproduction" rate. This can be defined by reference to the number of female children likely to be produced in the course of their lives by a thousand female babies if the present specific fertility and mortality rates remain unchanged. If any thousand female babies would exactly replace themselves by one thousand other female babies the rate is unity; if they would produce 1500 other female babies, the rate is 1.5; if only 800 female babies, the rate is 0.8. In a stationary population the rate would, of course, be unity; if the rate is 1.5 the population is likely to increase 50 per cent. in a generation. For England and Wales the net reproduction rate in the seventies was 1.5; by the turn of the century it was 1.3; by 1921 it was 1.1; by 1931, 0.8; by 1933, 0.7.[1]

Reference should also be made to the "gross repro-

[1] See Dr. Kuczynski's paper "The International Decline of Fertility" in *Political Arithmetic*, edited by Lancelot Hogben (London, 1938) for tables of net, and gross, reproduction rates at various dates in many countries.

duction rate". This is similar to the net reproduction rate except that it neglects mortality. It reflects the number of female babies which would be born in the course of their lives to a thousand female babies if they all survived to the end of the child bearing period. The significance of this measure is twofold: it provides a measure of the decline in fertility, and it indicates the maximum contribution that further reduction in mortality can make towards reversing the trend. For England and Wales the gross reproduction rate was 2.3 in 1870, the rate fell below unity in 1927, and was .9 in 1935. The decline in fertility has gone so far that no improvement of mortality will suffice to counteract it.

A similar conclusion to that reached by calculating the net reproduction rates may be reached by estimating the future population on the assumption that the existing conditions of fertility and mortality remain unchanged. Such an estimate has been made for England and Wales by Dr. Enid Charles.[1] Starting with the year 1931, and applying the present specific death rates (i.e. the number of deaths in each age group per thousand persons in that group), she estimates the number who will probably survive from each age group to replace those in the next age group at the later censuses. Similarly by applying the present specific fertility rates (i.e. the number of births to women in each age group per thousand women in that age group) she estimates the number of births in each decade. From the specific death rates for the early ages she then estimates the number of these

[1] See Dr. Charles's paper "The Effect of Present Trends in Fertility and Mortality upon the Future Population of Great Britain and upon its Age Composition," in *Political Arithmetic*.

babies which will survive to form the low age groups at succeeding censuses. An examination of the results of this calculation reveals that the conditions of fertility and mortality existing in 1931, when the population of England and Wales was 40 millions, would provide for some growth in the thirties, to 40.8 millions in 1940; for an almost stationary population in the forties, with a population of 40.7 millions in 1950; and for continuous and accelerating decline thereafter, to 37.3 millions in 1970, and to 28.5 millions in the year 2000.

These are estimates of what the population *would* be, *if* conditions of fertility and mortality had remained and were to continue as in 1931. In fact we know that through the thirties the decline in fertility continued, and that there was some, though less, decline in mortality. Dr. Charles therefore made another estimate based on the assumption of a further decline in fertility and mortality. This alternative assumption makes little difference to the estimate for 1940, but shows a substantial decline in the forties, and shows a population in 1970 of 33.8 millions (compared with 37.3 millions in the first estimate) and a population in the year 2000 of 17.7 millions (compared with 28.5 millions in the first estimate). One must consider the reasonableness of these assumptions. So far as the next thirty years is concerned the estimates are probably very reasonable. The attainment of a mean expectation of life of roughly 70 years by 1965 is a generous estimate which would only be fulfilled if there was continuous improvement in medical science and progressive elimination of conditions of serious poverty. The decline in fertility appears likely to continue; particularly until the class incidence of that decline has become completely generalized. When, however, the estimate goes beyond thirty years the element of uncertainty becomes very much bigger. The more obvious the trend of decline the more likely is the adoption of positive population policies calculated to reverse that trend; the longer the trend continues the more likely is the selection of *effective* population policies. The very publication of Dr. Charles's estimate becomes, therefore, a factor in changing the underlying assumptions on which it is based, and in making it probably an under estimate in the event, at least so far as the later years are concerned.

This pattern of population growth associated directly with the decline of mortality consequent on the development of scientific medicine, and indirectly with the increase in productivity resulting from the progressive application of science to agriculture and industry, is not peculiar to England and Wales, but is found to be common to all European countries. The dates at which growth began were generally later than in England, and later in the south and east than in the north and west. But of Europe as a whole we can say that the population in 1700 was probably no larger than in 1600, no larger, indeed, than in 1300; that the population did increase appreciably between 1700 and 1770; and that it is now three and a half times as big as in 1770. During this same period there was a migration of Europeans to other continents, which is estimated at some fifty millions. In Europe generally, as in England and Wales, this era of population growth seems to be approaching an end. The decline of fertility, evident in England after 1770 has become similarly evident in one country after another. In 1870 the gross reproduction rate exceeded 2 in every European country but France. By the turn of the century it was less than 2 in England and Sweden and had fallen to 1.5 in France. By 1910 it was below 2 in every country of Western and Northern Europe. By 1925 in only Russia, Poland, and the Balkans was the rate above 2, in the other countries of Europe the rate was between 1 and 1.5. In 1935 Russia was the only European country in which the rate exceeded 2, and it was below 1 in England, Norway, Sweden, Belgium, France, Austria, Switzerland, and Estonia. Dr. Kuczynski concludes that the gross reproduction rate for Western and Northern Europe was about 2 until 1890, and that it dropped below unity in 1931. In Central and Southern Europe it still exceeded 2 in 1922, but by 1935 had declined to 1.5.

This decline in fertility has in part been counteracted by a further decline in mortality; but with the gross reproduction rate less than unity no improvement in mortality can prevent a decline of population if the present low fertility rates continue. The prospect of decline is shown in the tables of net reproduction rates presented by Dr. Kuczynski. In Northern and Western Europe as a whole the net reproduction rate in 1870 was over 1.3, it had fallen by 1935 to 0.8. In Central and Southern Europe in 1935 it was 1.15. The rate is between 0.8 and 1 in such countries as Denmark, Czechoslovakia, Finland, France, Germany, Hungary,

Latvia, and Scotland; it is below 0.8 in Austria, Belgium, England, Estonia, Norway, Sweden, and Switzerland.

Nor is this pattern of growth and decline peculiar to Europe; in the United States a similar trend is found. The population of the United States grew at a spectacular pace before the Civil War, for six successive decades the average decennial increase was nearly 35 per cent. Since 1870 the growth has been slower, though still rapid by comparison with European countries. The decline in the rate of growth is due to a decline in immigration, and a decline in fertility partially counteracted by an improvement in mortality. With population declining in Europe it is not likely that immigration will again contribute much to population growth in the United States. The decline in fertility has already gone so far that the net reproduction rate is slightly below unity. In an excellent report on *Problems of a Changing Population*,[1] recently published by the United States government the conclusion is stated that "if no change occurred in the proportion of persons surviving from birth to different ages, or in fertility rates of women at different ages, population growth would gradually cease". And the report adds: "there is good reason to expect that further decline in fertility rates will be more rapid than the rise in survival rates". Even for the United States the end of the era of population growth is in sight; absolute decline is not likely to be evident before 1970, but in place of an increase of 16 millions in the twenties, the increase in the thirties

---

[1] *Report of the Committee on Population Problems to the National Resources Committee,* Washington, D.C., 1938.

will probably have been about 9 millions, in the forties will probably be less than 8 millions, and in the fifties less than 5 millions. Indeed one estimate, which does not appear to be based on very unlikely assumptions as to the trend of fertility would show the turning point, where absolute decline begins, as early as 1960.

The problems of declining population are in part problems of aging population, i.e., problems arising out of the increasing proportion of the population in the higher age groups which will be found in these declining populations. In England, for instance, the proportion of persons over 60 is now 11 per cent., by 1960 it is likely to be nearly 20 per cent., and in the population of the year 2000 as estimated by Dr. Charles the proportion would be 23 per cent. of her conservative estimate based on the continuance of present fertility rates, and 46 per cent. of her radical estimate based on the assumption of continued decline in fertility. This demonstrates the important point that the more rapid the decline, the more rapid the aging of the population. In the United States the proportion of the population over 65 is now about 6 per cent., but is expected to be about 15 per cent. by 1980.

II

I turn from the history and prediction of the facts of population growth, to opinions and ideas about the effect of such growth; to population problems and policies.

In the two or three centuries before the modern era of population growth began there was general ignorance of the actual trend, and general fear of decline.

The reason for this fear was largely military and political; the nation state needed man power to make it strong and influential. The economic reason is not, so far as I know, clearly stated in the mercantilist literature, but it is implied in the theory of exploitation expressed by John Bellers in "An Essay for Imploying the Able Poor" (1714): "Labouring people do raise and manufacture above double the food and clothing they use themselves"; were this not true "every gentleman must be a labourer and every idle man must starve." It would seem to follow that the more "labouring people" the better for the gentleman, the better for the state. I find support for this interpretation of the mercantilist population theory in a recent paper by Dr. Gunnar Myrdal: he described it as "a theory of the most advantageous exploitation".

The rapid growth of population after 1770 was barely recognized before it was the subject of apprehension. From Thomas Robert Malthus to John Stuart Mill economists talked of the danger of overpopulation, and preached doctrines of marital self restraint in the hope of averting the danger. Malthus did not see how the food supply could be increased as fast as population was increasing: Mill saw that the food supply could be increased fast enough, but thought that it could be done only at greatly increased human cost. But it was not only on economic grounds that Mill's attitude to the population problem was based, perhaps equally important were his political and ethical views on the emancipation of women. "A more important consideration still" he wrote to a friend, "is the perpetuation of the previous degradation of women, no alteration in which can be hoped for while their whole lives are devoted to the function of producing and rearing children.   That degradation and slavery is, in itself, so enormous an evil . . . that the limitation of the number of children would be, in my opinion, absolutely necessary to place human life on its proper footing even if there were subsistence for any number which could be produced."

It was clear to Mill that historically the returns to human effort in agriculture had been increasing as a result of improved technique.   The "progress of civilization" had partially counteracted the force of the static, but constantly operating, "law of diminishing returns".   We were better off, Mill would have us believe, as a result of this progress, but not as well off as we would have been had population not increased, and we were unwise to rely on continual technical progress.   This position was very generally accepted and curiously enough, persisted long after the beginning of the decline in the rate of growth, though the rate of scientific and technological progress was becoming more rapid.   How late the fear of overpopulation persisted can be shown by reference to Mr. Keynes's *Economic Consequences of the Peace Treaty* (1920): "Malthus disclosed a Devil.   For half a century all serious economical writings held that Devil in clear prospect.   For the next half century he was chained up and out of sight.   Now perhaps we have loosed him again."   Similarly in 1923 Mr. D. H. Robertson in a characteristically whimsical essay, "A word for the devil", wrote: "I do not in the name of the [Malthusian] devil, prophesy sudden cataclysm or even *necessarily* continued degradation: nevertheless in the pie of the world's poverty I detect his

smoky finger." To Mr. Robertson it appeared that
the standard of living in England "would have been
higher if there had been fewer of us." The vogue in
the twenties of E. M. East's *Mankind at the Cross-
roads* and E. A. Ross's *Standing Room Only,* is further
evidence of the persistence of this view.

Professor Edwin Cannan could never accept the
doctrine that increasing population necessarily meant
poverty. "Mill", he said, "coolly assumed that all the
improvements which have been made would have been
made just the same if the population had not grown.
We cannot assume that." This suggestion, that
progress in the arts is not unconnected with the
growth of population, leads to another, that effectively
to utilize the new arts you may need a bigger
population. To Cannan in England, and to Wicksell
in Sweden, must be attributed the idea which thus
develops, the idea of an optimum population. Over-
population thus came to mean that the population
was greater than the optimum size. The per capita
production of wealth in such circumstances could
be increased if the population could be reduced to
a size nearer thereto. But if it was reduced below this
optimum size, per capita production would again
decrease. Under-population was thus put on a par
with over-population; either involved, if not poverty,
at least less wealth than could be enjoyed with the
optimum population. It was recognized that the
optimum size changed with changing technology, and
it was fairly well agreed that modern machine industry
had in fact raised not merely the *possible* size of the
population, but also its *optimum* size. This concept
of the optimum population is elegant and, no doubt,

sound; unfortunately, however, we have not succeeded in developing adequate criteria for determining in any actual case either what is the optimum size, or even whether any particular population is too big or too small.

Quite recently the recognition of the probable decline of population has been followed by a complete reversal of our fears. We used to fear too rapid growth, we now fear decline; we would even be worried by the economic consequence of a stationary population, or of one growing too slowly. This new fear is not based on the belief that we are now near, or below, the optimum size. Those who think about the optimum at all probably feel that many countries in Europe are at present over-populated, and that some decline would be an advantage. Many of them, however, are worried because they can see no end to the decline short of extinction, just as Malthus and Mill could see no end of the increase short of "plague, pestilence and famine, battle, murder and sudden death". This particular worry need not detain us. We may note the comment of Professor Norman Himes in his review of *Political Arithmetic*: "A person of the intellectual power and originality of Dr. Enid Charles should know that she cannot reasonably and scientifically extrapolate a population trend for a century or more hence without allowing for new forces tending to restore equilibruim on a new level". We may suggest that the sociologist can explain this cycle of growth and decline in terms of slow social adjustment to two successive innovations, medicine and contraception; the second of which starting as a means of restoring

[1] *Journal of Political Economy*, October, 1939.

the equilibrium of birth and death rates which was upset by the first, became in the end a force making for a new disequilibrium.

The current fear of the economic consequences of a declining population, or even of a less rapidly growing one, is a by-product of the recent development of the theory of employment associated especially with Mr. J. M. Keynes. Both Mill, when discussing the inexorable law of diminishing returns, and Cannan, when explaining that we might be better off with a bigger rather than with a smaller population, assumed that there would be full employment in any case, or that the degree of employment was independent of the growth of the population. Some there were who thought that more people would mean greater unemployment. But generally the theory of employment was neglected. Modern economists have come to concern themselves properly, though perhaps too exclusively, with the problem of maintaining full employment, and they have become worried about the effect on employment of the process of decline, rather than about any fear of the disadvantage of a smaller population. For the maintenance of a high level of employment it has come to be recognized as necessary that there shall be adequate "investment" or "real capital formation". In the past the increase of population provided one of the most important sources of demand for new capital. Indeed, Professor Alvin Hansen has estimated that the growth of population in the nineteenth century was responsible for about 40 per cent. of the total volume of capital formation in western Europe, and for about 60 per cent. in the United States. In his presidential address to the American Economic Association in December, 1938, Professor Hansen stated the problem forcibly: "We are thus rapidly entering a world in which we must fall back upon a more rapid advance of technology than in the past if we are to find private investment opportunities adequate to maintain full employment . . . The great transition, incident to a rapid decline in population growth and its impact upon capital formation and the workability of a system of free enterprise, calls for high scientific adventure along all the fronts represented by the social science disciplines."

One is tempted to a "population interpretation" of modern capitalism. Professor Cannan sensed it. Professor J. R. Hicks now toys with it as he wonders in a footnote at the end of his *Value and Capital* whether the "whole industrial revolution of the last two centuries has been nothing else but a vast secular boom, largely induced by the unparalleled rise in population." Professor Schumpeter has little to say about population, yet perhaps the "first Schumpeter", as Dr. Innis in his review[1] of Schumpeter's recent *Business Cycles* has playfully christened the long cycle (1787-1929), was mainly conditioned by population growth; and it may prove to be the only "Schumpeter". Modern capitalist free enterprise may prove to have been a boom system, and the modern trend to something like the old mercantilism may be a trend towards institutions appropriate to an era of stationary population. We do not predict that there will be a declining population, but that population would decline unless some change takes place in the underlying

---

[1] *Canadian Journal of Economics and Political Science,* February, 1940.

conditions of fertility: similarly we do not predict that
there will be more unemployment if the population
does decline, but that there would be such unemployment unless there are changes in economic practice
and policy. Perhaps Mr. Keynes can show us how
to organize to meet the problem, perhaps the intensification of our difficulties will make us more receptive
to his instruction. Some of his followers already seem
inclined to exploit the new population fear to sell the
latest employment nostrum; in Mr. Reddaway's
Economics of a Declining Population,[1] for instance, one
wonders whether the primary interest is not in "consumers' dividends", in the manner, of course, of Meade,
not of Aberhart. This is one of the pleasant features
of the new population literature: with Malthus the
fear of over-population blocked all social reform; with
Myrdal the fear of depopulation becomes a "crowbar
for social reform", housing, public health, family allowances, education, all considered desirable in themselves
become so much more desirable as contributing, possibly, to maintenance of fertility.

We do not know whether the problem of unemployment was particularly severe in the seventeenth and
eighteenth centuries. The population was stationary
and technical progress slow, so that opportunities for
investment must have been limited. But total income
was small, so that saving was limited; and saving led
to the accumulation of things, the products of labour,
metallic money, plate, improvements to houses and
country estates. With the nineteenth century, as
income increased saving also increased; and saving
began to lead to the accumulation of promises to pay,

[1] London, 1939.

bank balances, paper securities, things which were not the products of labour. But the growth of population at home, and rapid technological progress combined with the opening of new continents to exploitation, provided enough investment to enable the system of free enterprise to function, if not perfectly, at least well enough to guarantee it against attack. In the modern world the "potential" national income[1] becomes bigger, and the volume of potential saving grows faster, while the accumulation of intangibles becomes the most general form of "pecuniary emulation". In these circumstances Professor Hansen tells us we must look to technological advance to provide new investment opportunities to make free enterprise "workable". However optimistic we may feel about the future of technology, we may well have misgivings as to its providing a solution for this particular problem. For one thing we must notice that all such technological progress increases the size of the potential income, still further increases saving and the need for investment. Secondly one must remember that rapid technological advance involves constant economic readjustment, increasing the uncertainty and the risk of investment. And such readjustment will be harder in a stationary or decreasing population, than it was in an increasing one. In an increasing population quite big changes in the relative importance of industries may, and did, occur without any industry actually declining: some would stop growing, others would grow more slowly, some would grow very

---

[1] I.e. the income that could be enjoyed if investment could be maintained on a level that would use up the savings which would be made out of the large income that we would enjoy if we could maintain full employment.

rapidly. In a declining population similar changes in the relative importance of industries will require an absolute shrinkage in some industries. Workers in the declining industries will be unemployed. Mr. H. D. Henderson stresses the future importance of this "structural unemployment".[1] Finally let us remember the warning of some sociologists that we cannot successfully adapt our social life to such constant and rapid change. Perhaps we need a century or two of stagnation to learn how to use the modern technology.[2] May I add that speculation in the effects of declining population is new, and that experience thereof is non-existent. We cannot be very confident in our anticipations either of troubles, or of remedies for the troubles.[3] Problems of aging complicate the problems of decline: perhaps this aging will increase the propensity to consume as the old live on their capital.

In many European countries positive populative policies have been adopted. Behind these policies lies generally the military and political interest in man-power for the totalitarian state. The usual elements in these policies are: (1) repressive legislation against abortion and contraception (Sweden is a notable exception, since along with a positive population policy goes state provision of birth control clinics); (2) special taxation of bachelors and provision of marriage loans (but in Germany these latter

[1] See his essay in *The Population Problem, the Experts and the Public*, London, 1938.

[2] Cf. R. E. Park, "Physics and Society", *Canadian Journal of Economics and Political Science*, May, 1940.

[3] For a more optimistic view see J. Jewkes in the *Manchester School*, October, 1929.

were intended, at first, to take women off the labour market); (3) family allowances (introduced in France on grounds of social justice but developed and adapted with special attention to their effects on population); (4) in Sweden housing policy has been used to promote population growth by provision of adequate room for larger families, by provision of collective creches to relieve the mothers, and by reduction of rent for large families; (5) in Germany an attempt is made to use the organs of propaganda to engender a spontaneous desire on the part of married couples to have numerous children. So far the effects of these policies have been negligible. "To increase fertility", says Dr. Kuczynski, "is a gigantic task. Fertility in the territory comprised by Western civilization is so low because most couples want few children. Even if the desire to raise children should not diminish farther, fertility, as a whole, is bound to decrease as the most efficient birth control devices are not universally known. A stop in the downward trend of fertility in the near future is to be expected only from an increasing desire to raise children, and a general desire for more children is hardly to be expected as long as public opinion in most countries does not favour population growth." Public opinion in this matter is changing; but it is one thing to believe that others should have bigger families, another thing to want a bigger family oneself. As Mr. T. H. Marshall says: "It is not only habits of thought that are weighted against the large family, but also the habitual organization of social life. The large family is not catered for, it does not fit into the scheme of things. Houses and flats get smaller, domestic help gets scarcer, holiday makers take to tents and to caravans . . . A man with children is spoken of as a man with encumbrances and treated as such."

There remains, of course, the possibility that the decline in fertility cannot be regarded as due solely, or even primarily to the operation of voluntary birth control. This is the view of that eminent biologist Raymond Pearl, and he is by no means alone in his belief. The extent of involuntary sterility requires investigation; if it is important we must rely on medicine to find means to remedy it. Medicine brought the death rate down, perhaps it will now bring the birth rate up.

I shall close this part of my lecture with a reference to the international politics of population, with special reference to the Nazi myth of living-space or *lebensraum*. The war of nerves involves a war of confidence in which ideas are munitions. The idea of "living-space" has an important place in the German armoury: its purpose is to build up confidence at home in the righteousness and reasonableness of German territorial claims, to undermine the confidence of the allies in the righteousness and reasonableness of resisting these claims, and to create in Germany an expectation that the unreasonable opposition to their reasonable claims will soon collapse. Hence the importance of the pamphlet by Dr. Kuczynski, *Living Space and Population Problems* (one of the Oxford Pamphlets on World Affairs) in which this particular myth is deflated by reference to the probable trend of population growth in Germany. Dr. Kuczynski quotes a statement of Herr Goebbels: "It is a pity that the

Western Powers conduct an ostrich policy in the matter of colonies. Do they think that fifty years hence, when the 80,000,000 Germans will be 130,000,000, the earth can remain distributed as at present." He might have quoted the more extravagant statement of Herr Hitler in *Mein Kampf*: "The rightness of that foreign policy can only be recognized in a bare century's time, if by then 250 million Germans are living on this continent." To such extravagant claims for living space for the teeming population of the future Germany Dr. Kuczynski replies with an estimate of the probable population of Germany (including Austria) made by the German Statistical Office. This estimate is based on rather more favourable assumptions as to the trend of fertility and mortality than are the similar estimates for the other countries. Yet the conclusion is reached that the total population may be expected to increase from 75 millions in 1940 to but 80 millions in 1970, and then to decrease to 77 millions by the year 2000. If there is to be a problem of living space for an expanding German population, that problem will be the product of their own population policies. It seems, at present, unlikely that these policies will even seriously retard the decline in fertility.

But if the knowledge of the approach of declining population dispels the myth of living space, it creates a new problem which may also appear soluble in terms of territorial acquisition. For, if declining population threatens increasing unemployment, colonies may be coveted as an outlet for investment rather than as an outlet for population. In estimating the prospects for enduring peace in the future, and in engineering an immediate peace settlement after this war, a realistic apprehension of the economic stresses of declining population is of real importance. And may I here express my surprise, and horror, that at the round table on demographic questions at the International Studies Conference on Peaceful Change in 1937, when the supposedly over-populated countries of Europe cast envious eyes on the supposedly under-populated countries such as Canada, there was almost no reference to the prospect of population decline in Europe. At that conference Professor Carr-Saunders stated his belief that, unless the population of the lightly populated countries increases at a rate of 20 per cent. per decade, the charge that "the owners occupy territory that they do not use" would be justified. How slight are the prospects for growth at such a rate in Canada will be indicated in Part III. The living space myth is a dangerous one for Canadians.

III

At last I come to Canada. Here popular interest centres on one question, namely the advisability of promoting immigration. The economists are almost unanimous in opposing any vigorous immigration policy, though Stephen Leacock in his *Economic Prosperity in the British Empire* stated his belief that the resources of Canada would support a population of 250 millions. Perhaps the humorist trespassed momentarily on the territory of the economist! The political support for active immigration policy comes from the transportation companies, imperialist groups, and the normal "boosting" psychology of the frontier. It is on this immigration issue that I might reasonably be expected to pronounce in this paper. But for one who agrees with the majority of his colleagues in opposing any considerable immigration in the near future, I have recklessly handicapped myself in the last part of my lecture. I have asserted that there is no test of under- or over-population, thus depriving myself of a weapon of defence; and I have emphasized the advantages of rapid growth of population for the workability of free enterprise, thus providing a weapon of offence to my opponents. I will now add another handicap: economists can predict with reasonable success the probable effect of small changes in an otherwise regular development, they cannot predict the effect of cataclysmic change, in fact they are often late in recognizing its effects. In what follows, then, I shall be talking of what may be expected if Canada continues to depend very largely on the export of staples. What her population could be, or should be, in an era of autarky, I shall not stop to consider.

The population of Canada has grown from two and a half millions in 1841, to ten and a half millions in 1931. This growth has not been even: in the fifties the decennial rate of increase was 33 per cent.; in the next four decades the rate of growth was much smaller and declining; it averaged 13 per cent. and had fallen to 11 per cent. by the end of the century. In the first decade of this century the rate of growth was again 33 per cent., but it declined to 22 per cent. in the decade 1911-21, and to 18 per cent. in the twenties. Until the census has been taken next year we cannot know what the rate of growth was in the thirties, but it will probably prove to have been 11 per cent.

The growth of wealth, and of population, in a pioneer country will necessarily be slow unless there emerges some staple commodity for export.[1] With no such staple exports the emergence of a surplus above necessary food supplies would be slow, the accumulation of capital equipment would be almost impossible. With the development of an export staple a surplus emerges: a higher standard of living is established on the basis of imported manufactures and some capital equipment can be purchased with the surplus funds. But even this surplus would be small, and would only provide for slow growth: rapid growth is dependent on capital imports, which again are dependent on the existence of a staple export to provide for interest payments on the debt thus incurred. The conditions favourable to rapid growth in a pioneer country are, then, high prices for its staple exports and availability of foreign loans at low interest rates. These conditions were fulfilled in the two decades 1851-61, and 1901-11. In the former period the prices of lumber, wheat and fish were rising; European funds were available at low rates for railway building and other construction; European population growth promised an increasing demand for food and raw materials while progressive industrialization reduced the proportion growing food. World conditions remained favourable till 1875, but Canadian growth lagged: Ontario farm lands were

[1] See W. A. Mackintosh, "Some Aspects of a Pioneer Economy", *Canadian Journal of Economics and Political Science*, November, 1936.

mostly occupied by 1860, and the Homestead Act of 1862 was a prelude to the opening up of the American West. There followed twenty years of falling prices and general depression (1875-95): the prices of Canadian exports fell and large scale borrowing was impossible. The upturn in prices, and improvement in prosperity which began about 1896 brought a new period of expansion in Canada. The prices of her staple exports were rising, and particularly important was the rising price of wheat. There was renewed interest in foreign investment, and in Canada as a borrower: funds were available at low rates, and steel was cheap as a result of technological advance. Western settlement in the United States was nearly complete; and the essential technical problems of wheat production in the Canadian prairie had been solved with the invention of the chilled steel plough, with the development of dry farming practice, with the selection of early maturing wheat, with the completion of the transcontinental railway, and the establishment of lines of elevators. The rapid growth of the Canadian West in the decade 1901-11 is not, then, surprising. But it is important to notice the stimulating effect of Western expansion on other parts of Canada; prairie farmers bought lumber from British Columbia and manufactures from Ontario and Quebec. There was, therefore, general Canadian expansion: but the impetus came from Europe.

The lack of comprehensive and comparable vital statistics prior to 1921, and the lack of any adequate statistics of emigration, make it difficult to determine how far the Canadian population has grown by natural increase, and how far by net immigration. It is necessary, nevertheless, to make some attempt to describe the pattern of past growth in order to throw light on the probable pattern of future growth.

During the last century mortality has probably declined in Canada as in other countries; the crude death rate fell from 11 per thousand in the early twenties to 9 per thousand in the early thirties. This rate is very low as compared with other countries owing to the very favourable age composition: the mean expectation of life, on the other hand was, in 1931, 59 years, or slightly lower than in England and Wales. Infant mortality has been greatly reduced, from 102 per thousand live births in 1921, to 66 in 1935. Further improvement may be expected in the next decade especially if the high rates of Quebec and New Brunswick (83 and 77 respectively) are brought into line with those of the other provinces. But though further decline in mortality may be expected, an increasing proportion of older people in the population over the next few decades will be working to maintain, or even raise, the crude death rate.

Fertility, too, has declined in Canada as in other countries. In the absence of records of births Professor Burton Hurd[1] has used census materials to show the trend of birth rates. He shows a decline in the number of children aged 0-4 per 1000 women aged 15-45 from 614 in 1881 to 467 in 1931. The decline has not been even: this proportion fell to 535 in 1901, recovered to 566 in 1911, and then again declined. This rise in

[1] "The Decline in the Canadian Birth Rate", *Canadian Journal of Economics and Political Science*, November, 1936.

1901-11 may, however, have been due to the influx of early marrying, high-fertility, peoples from Central and Eastern Europe during the early years of the decade.

Dr. Woodbury[1] suggests the possibility that the apparent buoyancy in the rate of increase of the Canadian born in the decade 1901-11 may be the result of incomplete ennumeration in 1901 in the sparsely populated districts of the West. It would be most useful to be more certain on this point. We want to know whether Canadian natural increase responded to the stimulus of economic expansion, and whether it is likely so to respond again. My own view is that such response is unlikely, but the evidence is slim and inconclusive. Looking forward, it seems unlikely that the trend to lower fertility will be reversed in the near future: this is suggested by the history of other countries, by the belief that the existing differential fertilities between classes and regions will steadily diminish as the influences making for lower fertility become more generally felt, and by the belief that future expansion is more likely to be urban and industrial and thus likely to strengthen the influences making for lower fertility. In this connection it is of interest to notice that Professor Hurd found evidence of differential fertility between urban and rural groups, and between large and small towns, both in English and in French Canada. The number of children 0-4 per 1000 women 15-44 in Canada in 1931 was 480 for the rural English, 362 for the English in cities of 1000 to 30,000 persons, and 298 for the English in cities over

[1] In a review of the Canadian Census of 1931 in the *Canadian Journal of Economics and Political Science,* February, 1940.

30,000: it was 751 for the rural French, 543 for the French in cities with from 1,000 to 30,000 persons, and 429 for the French in cities over 30,000.

What, then, are the prospects for future population growth in Canada, by natural increase? With then existing fertility and mortality rates the net reproduction rate in 1931 was 1.3 for Canada as a whole. There were, however, wide differences between provinces: New Brunswick, with a rate of 1.6, and Quebec and Saskatchewan, with rates of 1.5, were at the top of the list; Manitoba, with a rate of 1.2, Ontario with a rate of 1.1, and British Columbia with a rate of 0.9, were the provinces with rates less than the general rate. If the decline in fertility continues, as I believe it will in the next twenty or thirty years, especially in what are now the high fertility regions, the moderate rate of growth through natural increase promised by a reproduction rate of 1.3, is unlikely to be achieved.

Professor Hurd[1] has calculated the future population in Canada, by quinquennial years from 1931 to 1971, which would be found if there were no further immigration, and if fertility rates remained as in the period 1931-36, and if the mortality rates of the 1931 Life Tables remained unchanged. The projection shows a population for 1971 of 15.4 millions. This is a considerable absolute increase, but the rate of growth would be small as compared with the previous thirty years, and would be decreasing. The decennial percentage increases of population for the decades 1901-31 were: 33, 22 and 18; the percentage increases according

1 "Some Implications of Prospective Population Changes in Canada", *Canadian Journal of Economics and Political Science*, November, 1939.

to Professor Hurd's projection for the decades 1931-71 would be: 11, 11, 9.5, 8. This projection, like that of Dr. Charles for England, shows what would happen if the fertility and mortality rates did not change. Professor Hurd feels that the fertility rates on which his estimate was based were abnormally low as a result of postponement of marriage in the depression; he therefore doubts whether future decline .in fertility before 1971 will be greater than can be counteracted by the further decline in mortality. To me it seems more than likely, however, that the natural increase in Canada in the next thirty years will be less than is there shown.

Professor Hurd explains that his projection "indicates what will happen to our population if we remain on a substantially self-contained basis populationwise, and natural increase continues at about its present level". "Departures", he goes on to say, "are bound to occur because of unpredictable changes in the underlying economic, social and political forces controlling population growth and population movements. For example, throttling of international trade could hardly fail to depress the birth rate, while a lowering of barriers might well have the opposite effect. Some revolutionary change in the technique of production, the discovery of important new resources or of ways of profitably using potential resources might materially change the population picture." I agree that revolutionary changes in production, the emergence of new staples, for example, will profoundly affect population movement, and I turn next to discuss the prospects for growth by immigration. I feel less confident that the trend of growth by natural increase would be seriously affected by changes in productivity. European population history does not suggest that growth is a response to increased productivity, nor that decline is a response to decreased productivity. Canadian population statistics suggest that fertility did increase in the decade 1901-11; but there is, as I have already indicated, some reason to doubt this; and the social conditions in a wheat economy, rather than increased prosperity, may have been the cause of the increase, if any. Later staples were produced under conditions less favourable to fertility—pulp and paper, and minerals. Who knows what the next staple will be?

As a preliminary to discussion of the prospects of growth through immigration some account of the contribution of immigration in the first thirty years of the century is necessary. According to estimates of the Dominion Statistician (and in the absence of adequate vital statistics and statistics of emigration, a good deal of estimating is necessary) there was between 1901 and 1931 a natural increase of 3.3 millions, and an immigration of 5.1 millions, which might have added 8.4 millions to the population. The actual increase in population was only 5 millions; 3.4 millions must therefore have emigrated. What we lost was probably half a million Canadian born, and three of the five million immigrants. This leads to four reflections, or questions. First, there are those who believe that this heavy immigration depressed the birth rate, that we grew no faster, or little faster, than if there had been no immigration, that we substituted, in Mr. Gilbert Jackson's phrase, "the colonist car for the cradle". Whether this is true cannot be determined. It depends on whether opportunities for the Canadian born were reduced by the competition of immigrants for jobs, and on whether fertility is really responsive to current earnings of parents and prospective earnings of children. My own view, for what it is worth, is that there was a considerable net addition to the population through immigration, that the Canadian birth rate was not depressed thereby, and that the emigration of Canadians to the United States would have been in any case considerable. Second, it is of some significance that in the decade 1901-11, with most favourable conditions for growth and with a flood of immigrants arriving at our shores, the average annual increase was 180,000. In the next two decades, with the stimulus of war production and the emergence of new staples, the average yearly increase was 160,000. It is hard to envisage a greater absolute increase as feasible in the next few decades particularly in the face of declining population in Europe: such a decline involves a reduced consumption of certain staples; it also involves a condition of general depression, unfavourable for the prices of staples, unless or until new economic policies appropriate to decline have been devised and adopted, and among the policies likely to be adopted at an early stage are policies of economic nationalism which make more difficult the rôle of the staple exporter. Third, it is important to remember that we have experience only of rapid immigration in a period when there was a safety valve, namely an open door to the United States. We have no experience by which to judge the effect on our standard of living of large scale immigration at a time when expansion in our export trade is difficult. We should hesitate before making the experiment. With our economy geared to export trade the optimum rate of growth for Canada seems to be dependent on factors outside Canada. Finally, even if we want immigrants, it is doubtful whether the countries of Europe from which we would like to select them will be willing to lose population to us. The "struggle for population" has begun. All of which leads me to the conclusion that Canadian population will not increase in the next thirty years faster than, if as fast as, Professor Hurd's projection suggests.

If Europe is unable to counteract the depressive influences of decline, or if to counteract them Europe has to adopt nationalistic policies, Canada will face difficulties. For depression in Europe has always been transmitted to Canada through low prices of staple commodities, and through cessation of foreign lending. This latter may become less important as we attain economic maturity. Further, our optimum rate of population growth has been and probably will for some decades to come be affected by these conditions in Europe, and, I should add, the United States: and our rapid growth in favourable periods has been, probably had to be, through contributions from Europe's population growth. Slower growth in Canada may mean inadequate investment opportunities even to take care of the growing volume of "potential" Canadian saving. The prospects for Canadian prosperity in the era of population decline are gloomy. But the approach of such difficulties may produce a population policy intended to change the trend, and may lead to changes in our economic system calculated to meet the new strain. It is doubtful whether a Canadian population policy can help while the European decline is unchecked. But if there is to be a population policy, may an immigrant admirer of the native stock suggest that it be directed to reducing mortality and increasing fertility at home. And we do not need to be entirely dependent on a European solution of the economic problem; their solution of their own problem may injure us, or their solution may prove inappropriate for us, or they may find no solution. We in Canada are faced with the necessity of adapting our economy, and our conceptions of economic policy, to life in a different world from that of the nineteenth century. One of the most important differences is that discussed in this lecture.

V. CANADA AND THE LAST WAR
by F. H. UNDERHILL

NO attempt will be made here to deal with all the topics that are suggested by the title "Canada and the Last War". My paper is confined to two main themes: (1) the development of the relations between Canada and Great Britain as affected by the war; (2) the war effort itself, the raising of troops, the production of munitions, the fighting overseas, and the political difficulties at home produced by this effort.

I. CANADA'S RELATIONS WITH GREAT BRITAIN

In 1914 Canada was about to celebrate the achievement of one hundred years of peace with her only neighbour. On Christmas eve, 1914, it would be one hundred years since the signing of the Treaty of Ghent had brought to an end the last war with an external enemy in which British North Americans had been engaged. Since that time the colonies had expanded and had united themselves into the Dominion of Canada in a long peaceful evolution during which they had lived for the most part sheltered from the impact of European power politics and European wars.

In 1885 Sir John Macdonald had declined an invitation to send an official Canadian force to assist in the British Soudan expedition up the Nile "to get Gladstone and Co.", as he put it, "out of the hole they have plunged themselves into by their own imbecility."[1]

In 1899 Sir Wilfrid Laurier would no doubt have preferred to make a similar reply to the suggestions that he send a Canadian force to another war in Africa—in South Africa this time. Mr. Chamberlain in the Colonial Office had been pressing vigorously to get colonial support for British policy; and when the war started he declined individual offers of help from Canadians because he wanted an official offer from the government such as would commit it to the principle of imperial solidarity against external enemies. In the end Laurier found himself forced to take action not so much by pressure from Colonial Office or Governor-General as by pressure from English-speaking Canada; and ten days after the war broke out, without parliamentary authority, he passed an Order-in-Council providing for the raising and sending of a force. This action, according to the safeguarding clause at the end of the Order-in-Council, was not to be taken as a precedent. "The precedent, Mr. Prime Minister", retorted Henri Bourassa, "is the accomplished fact." And in spite of Laurier's denial that any change was made in 1899 in Canada's relations with Great Britain, the precedent of the accomplished fact has operated ever since. The Boer War marks the turning point in the evolution of Canada's military position in the Empire and the world at large.

After the Boer War Laurier became more and more wary about entanglements in British military adventures. He defeated all efforts towards any form of centralized control and direction of imperial policy;

[1] Sir Joseph Pope, *Correspondence of Sir John Macdonald*, p. 338.

and his achievements in this field have been duly celebrated by his biographers, Dr. Skelton and Mr. Dafoe. But in English-speaking Canada our participation in the Boer War undoubtedly stimulated imperial enthusiasm, and Laurier's policy of North American aloofness from what he called "the vortex of European militarism" met with criticism from all those who were attracted by the vision of a Canada playing her part in world affairs as a junior partner in the great British firm, all those who regarded 1899 as the end of the era of parochial colonialism, to whom our first participation in overseas military efforts marked, as John Buchan was later to put it in his *Life of Lord Minto*, "a spiritual enlargement."

These issues did not occupy the centre of Canadian politics during the years of the great boom which set in after 1900, but they were pushed to the centre when the naval scare of 1909 started a long controversy over Canada's naval policy and her responsibilities in imperial defence, a controversy that was still going on when the Great War broke out in 1914.

Laurier's Naval Bill of 1910 provided for the building and maintenance of a Canadian naval force under the control of the Canadian government, a force which might be put at the disposal of the British Admiralty in case of war. "If England is at war, we are at war", he announced. "I do not say that we shall always be attacked, neither do I say that we would take part in all the wars of England. That is a matter that must be decided by circumstances".

His bill was opposed by the Tory loyalists who made up the majority of the Conservative opposition on the ground that the only worth-while thing which Canada could do to help Britain in this hour of crisis was to make a cash contribution to the British navy. It was opposed by the Conservative leader with rather more subtle and complex arguments, which are important to grasp because the stand which Mr. Borden took now was to be maintained by him to the end of his career. Borden was a nationalist as well as Laurier. He agreed with the principle of a Canadian navy; and in 1918 when the great war was over he was to lead the Dominion prime ministers in rejecting Lord Jellicoe's scheme of a unitary centralized navy for the whole Empire. But in 1910 he was critical of the isolationist implications which he professed to discern in the policy of the Liberals. "Canada", he declared in a phrase which he was often to repeat in later years, "cannot be a hermit nation." He advocated his party's policy of a contribution to the British navy as an immediate emergency policy, but he went on to add that if Canada was to share in the expenses of British policy, she must be given a voice in shaping that policy. When he came into office after the 1911 election he quashed the Laurier programme of a separate Canadian navy and introduced his own bill for the raising of $35,000,000 as a gift to build three dreadnoughts for the British navy. This, he explained, was only an emergency policy. Canada should not decide on her final defence measures till she had discussed and reached a conclusion with Great Britain on the question of the control of foreign policy.

Borden's bill was defeated in the Senate. The Liberal majority in the Senate were obviously trying to force an appeal to the people by throwing out a major measure of governmental legislation. But by this time it was 1913, the great boom had burst, and Canadian governments do not, if they can avoid it, have recourse to general elections when times are bad. Borden accepted his defeat and dropped the subject. So, when the war broke out in 1914, the Canadian people had not yet made up their minds what their permanent defence policy in relation to the Empire ought to be.

The line which Borden adopted on the naval question in these years was partly devised to meet the situation in Quebec. His emergency contribution was to satisfy the loyalists in Ontario, his insistence that ultimate policy was not yet being decided upon was to quiet the alarm of Quebec nationalism. Laurier's proposal to start building a navy had roused the Quebec nationalists under Bourassa against him. Ever since the Boer War Bourassa had been sniping at Laurier for betraying the French Canadians to British imperialism. Now he launched a full attack. In the famous Drummond-Arthabaska by-election, fought in 1910, a nationalist candidate defeated the official Liberal, and Laurier from that moment was plagued by a growing movement in his own province against every step that could be interpreted as an entanglement in overseas British wars.

In the general election of 1911 Conservatives and Nationalists in Quebec made arrangements for co-operation in the constituencies, and it was the seats which they won from Laurier in this way that drove him from office. The Quebec Nationalists were given their share of seats in the Borden cabinet. In 1915 one of these seats was held by a gentleman who had distinguished himself on the election platform by a declaration that he would like to shoot holes in the union jack in order that the breeze of liberty might blow through it. Much of the tragedy of the 1917-18 conscription crisis in Quebec dates from these events in 1910-11. It was this deliberate encouragement of extreme anti-British feeling in Quebec followed by the persistent misunderstanding of Quebec nationalist sentiment by the government after 1914 which laid the foundation of the violent bitterness of feeling in that province in the later years of the war. Surely historians have been unduly tender to Sir Robert Borden on this issue.

At the moment of the outbreak of the war, however, all groups in the Canadian community accepted the fact of automatic Canadian participation wholeheartedly. Laurier had always declared that if Britain were ever engaged in a life-and-death struggle it would be Canada's duty to come to her assistance; and he now gave the government his support in their task of mobilizing national action. The whole weakness of Laurier's advocacy of Canadian autonomy before 1914 had in fact consisted in this very point, that in the delicate balance of power in Europe a life-and-death struggle was the only kind of war which was likely, and that therefore Canada was automatically committed to all the results of British policy, however much the pose of aloof autonomy might be kept up. Borden had seen this clearly and accordingly demanded a voice in the making of that British policy. His demand met with little response from the British government before 1914, but he continued to make it; and after August 4th, with Canada's magnificent contributions in men, munitions, and money, his demand became unanswerable.

From August, 1914, the Borden conception of Canada's position in the Empire seemed completely to have displaced that of Laurier. It was not in Canada for the moment that Sir Robert had difficulty in getting his ideas accepted but in England. For two years there he met with frequent causes of exasperation in the lack of imagination with which the British authorities greeted the Canadian effort. Expressions of gratitude he received in abundance. But he was not admitted into the *arcana imperii*. Far from being consulted by them about general policy, he could not even get satisfactory information from the British authorities about what was going on. He found much verbal sympathy with his demand that Canada be given a share in foreign policy but no practical action. Bonar Law, the secretary for the colonies, replied to his representations in a letter which is worth quoting (November 3, 1915, to Sir G. Perley, Canadian High Commissioner):

We fully realize the great part which your government is playing in this war, and as Sir Robert Borden found when he was here we were only too delighted to put him into possession of all the information which was available to the cabinet. . . As regards the question of consultation, here again I fully recognize the right of the Canadian government to have some share in a war in which Canada is playing so big a part. I am, however, not able to see any way in which this could be practically done . . . If no scheme is practicable then it is very undesirable that the question should be raised.

Sir Robert retorted in forceful language (letter to Perley, January 6, 1916):

During the past four months since my return from Great Britain, the Canadian government (except for an occasional telegram from you or Sir Max Aitken) have had just what information could be gleaned from the daily press and no more. As to consultation, plans of campaign have been made and unmade, measures adopted and apparently abandoned and generally speaking steps of the most important and even vital character have been taken, postponed or rejected without the slightest consultation with the authorities of this Dominion. It can hardly be expected that we shall put 400,000 or 500,000 men in the field and willingly accept the position of having no more voice and receiving no more consideration than if we were toy automata. Any person cherishing such an expectation harbours an unfortunate and even dangerous delusion. Is this war being waged by the United Kingdom alone, or is it a war waged by the whole Empire?[1]

This was in January, 1916, when the war had been in progress for a year and a half. It was not until the end of that year that Sir Robert finally achieved for his country the practical recognition of its right to a voice in the making of policy. And one may doubt whether he would not have had to wait still longer had not the coalition of the leisurely Asquith and the negative Bonar Law been replaced by the dynamic leadership of Mr. Lloyd George, who straightway invited the Dominion prime ministers to sit in the war cabinet which he set up on becoming prime minister of Britain. Whatever we may think of Mr. Lloyd George's fondness for political intrigue, and whatever feelings we may have about the coarsening quality of his liberalism as the war years went on, there is no doubt that his succession to the prime ministership was of tremendous significance for the

[1] This correspondence is quoted from *Robert Laird Borden: His Memoirs* (cited hereafter as *Borden Memoirs*), Vol. II, pp. 621, 622.

Dominions. Here at last was a man in charge who didn't wear the old school tie, whose quick intuitive mind saw at once the value of the Dominion's contribution both to the total war effort and to his own particular aims.

One senses in reading his *Memoirs* that one of his motives for giving the Dominions a share in policy was that of calling in the vigorous unspent energies of the New World to redress the balance of the Old, where war weariness by the end of 1916 was already a serious difficulty and where the air was thick with proposals for an early peace. Another motive is undoubted. As he told Borden in 1918, he especially wanted the support of the Dominion prime ministers to strengthen him in dealing with the generals, whose unimaginative war of attrition on the western front seemed to him a disastrous policy.[1] Sir Robert certainly was enthusiastically with him in this cause. He had learnt from Sir Arthur Currie what the strategy of British G.H.Q. and the tactics of the British army commanders had cost the Canadian troops on the Somme. Currie had told him that the British Intelligence was so bad that he had given up reading their reports.[2] Nevertheless, the generals remained in control. The sacrifices of 1916 on the Somme were followed by those of 1917 at Passchendaele. Mr. Lloyd George tells how he sent General Smuts and Sir Maurice Hankey on a confidential tour of the western front to see if they could unearth for him any promising generals in place of the Haig-Robertson combination. They spied out the land

[1] *Borden Memoirs*, Vol. II, p. 827.
[2] *Ibid.*, p. 811.

but reported no success.[1] Why did Sir Robert not tell him about the qualities of Currie?

Sir Robert was in England from February to May in 1917 taking part in the deliberations of the Imperial War Cabinet and of the Imperial War Conference, and again during June, July, and part of August in 1918. After he returned to Canada on this occasion he was hastily summoned back to London by Mr. Lloyd George in October and arrived just after the Armistice. The Imperial War Cabinet, having discussed all aspects of its peace policy, then transferred itself bodily to Paris in January 1919, as the British Empire Delegation, and here the Canadian delegates spent a busy six months until the treaty with Germany was finally signed.

In the famous Orpen painting of the signing of the peace treaties the *homunculi*, Allied and German, who sit or stand around the table, are dwarfed by the enormous arches of the Hall of Mirrors, and over them near the ceiling towers the inscription "Le Roi gouverne par lui même". To us looking backward now it seems that the king who governed by himself during those years from 1914 to 1919 was named Chaos. But Sir Robert and his associates at the time thought that they could discern a pattern in these events, a pattern which they themselves had traced. And the pattern was the achievement by the Dominions of national status. The Imperial War Cabinet, the membership in the Peace Conference, the signing by Canadians of the peace treaties, the entry by Canada as an original member into the League of Nations and the International Labour

[1] David Lloyd George, *War Memoirs*, Vol. IV, p. 2267.

Organization—did not all these things signify a new position for Canada in the Empire and in the world at large?

But how much was really achieved by the device of the War Cabinet towards a permanent solution of the problem of the proper form of co-operation among governments who had agreed to pool their resources in a common cause? Or had they finally agreed to pool their resources? Canadian participation in the inner discussions on policy was effective only when the Canadian prime minister was present in Europe, which was only for a few months each year. The Canadian prime minister moreover was largely dependent for his information about and his interpretation of events upon British officials rather than upon his own Canadian officials; he had, in fact, very few of these latter with him.

Sir Robert Borden's own *Memoirs* are so full of his pride in the winning of full recognition for Canada's new national status that he has very little space left to tell us about the other subject on which we would like enlightenment—i.e. the policy he pursued on all the specific issues that arose in London in 1917 and 1918 before the Armistice and in London and Paris during the period of treaty making. In the long run policy is much more important than status. We get more information from Mr. Lloyd George's *Memoirs* and from the scattered references to Canada in other English and American books than we do from the Canadian prime minister. And on the whole it must be agreed that the information is highly creditable to the leaders who spoke and acted for Canada during these momentous months.

In the War Cabinet Sir Robert opposed all ambitions for annexing enemy territory. He was sceptical about the fantastic schemes for trying and condemning the Kaiser. He joined with Mr. Lloyd George in opposing armed intervention by the Allies against the Soviet government in Russia. When anti-Wilsonian and anti-American views were being expressed he intervened with a downright exposition of Canada's attitude: "he would regret if we entered the Peace Conference with any feeling of antagonism towards the United States. . . . If the future policy of the British Empire meant working in co-operation with some European nation [i.e. France] against the United States, that policy could not reckon on the approval or support of Canada. Canada's view was that as an Empire we should keep clear, as far as possible, of European complications and alliances. This feeling had been strengthened by the experience of the war, into which we had been drawn by old-standing pledges and more recent understandings, of which the Dominions had been not even aware."[1] Note how the essential North American attitude of Canada crops up even when her Prime Minister is in the midst of activities which have carried her furthest from North American aloofness.

At Paris Sir Robert had to maintain the solidarity of the British Dominions by backing Australia and South Africa in their demands for German colonies. But in the famous meeting of the Big Four at which the Dominion "cannibals" presented their case he seems to have damned it with faint praise. At any rate, on the testimony both of Mr. Lloyd George and

[1] David Lloyd George, *The Truth About the Peace Treaties*, p. 198.

Mr. Churchill, Borden's influence behind the scenes was one of the main factors in restraining the other Dominions from forcing a deadlock on the subject of colonies.[1] Perhaps this in itself amounts to only faint praise for Canada's record, since there were no German colonies in the North Atlantic or Pacific to excite our Canadian cupidity. The Canadian prime minister, however, undoubtedly made a good impression on everyone who has recorded his impressions, and in this respect he was in striking contrast to Mr. Hughes of Australia who made a uniformly bad impression on everyone. The now famous Borden memorandum criticizing Article X of the Covenant is declared by David Hunter Miller, the legal expert of the American delegation, to have been the most effective presented at Paris.[2] Sir Robert served on the Commission which delimited the boundaries of Greece and Serbia; and Mr. Harold Nicolson has nothing but praise for the intelligence and diligence with which he mastered the intricate details organized for him by the expert official of the Foreign Office who in this case was Nicolson himself.[3] Professor Shotwell is not quite so complimentary about the Canadian record on the setting up of the International Labour Organization. Borden was extremely obstinate and made trouble until Canada's position in the I.L.O. was settled as being on a par with her position in the League of Nations. Here again it was Canadian status rather than policy in which he seems to have

[1] D. Lloyd George, op. cit., p. 538; W. Churchill, The Aftermath, p. 153.
[2] David Hunter Miller in his lecture in the volume edited by House and Seymour, What Really Happened at Paris.
[3] Harold Nicolson, Peacemaking, 1919; p. 259.

have been interested; and Professor Shotwell, who along with Gompers of the U.S.A. and Barnes of Great Britain was trying to achieve an international recognition of Labour's importance in the world, reports little appreciation of this point of view in the Canadian delegation.[1]

On economic and financial questions the chief Canadian spokesman was Sir George Foster. The War Cabinet set up a committee to consider reparations, of which Hughes of Australia was chairman. "To counterbalance his optimism", Mr. Lloyd George tells us, "I added the name of Sir George Foster, a statesman of recognized sanity and moderation."[2] Foster was shocked at the fantastic calculations produced by British bankers on the committee as to Germany's capacity to pay reparations. "It was all guesswork and sentiment", he confided to his diary, "we shall bring in a report but it will be based on extremely little real evidence."[3] Mr. Lloyd George regarded the committee's report as "a wild and fantastic chimera"[4] (as did Mr. J. M. Keynes), but it was, alas, from this chimera that the ultimate reparations clauses of the Peace Treaty originated.

Sir Robert Borden himself returned from Europe in a state of mind somewhat altered from the high confidence and exaltation with which he had carried the Dominion into the war in 1914. "Of those who took part in the Peace Conference", he told his audience in the University of Toronto at the Marfleet lectures

[1] J. T. Shotwell, *At the Paris Peace Conference.*
[2] D. Lloyd George, *The Truth about the Peace Treaties*, p. 459.
[3] W. S. Wallace, *The Memoirs of Rt. Hon. Sir George Foster*, pp. 193, 194.
[4] D. Lloyd George, *op. cit.*, p. 461.

in October 1921, "some at least returned to this continent with a sense of depression. The fierce antagonisms, the ancient hatreds and the bitter jealousies of the European nationals there assembled were not inspiring."[1] Yet whatever his disillusionment about the prospect of a permanent settlement of Europe as a whole, he had no doubts about the permanence of the work of himself and his fellow Britannic statesmen in reconstituting the structure of the British Empire. One fundamental thing they had achieved, and that was the new 1917 Borden-Smuts Commonwealth of six nation-states, all equal in status, all together pursuing a common foreign policy—not, as before 1914, a policy carried out by the British Foreign Office acting as a sort of trustee on behalf of colonies who were still minors; not, as proposed by the Round Tableites and other federationists, a policy made by some new central imperial parliament and executive; but a policy worked out in common by independent governments through continuous consultation. He looked forward to a constitutional conference after the war which would regularize and systematize this *ad hoc* machinery of War Cabinet and British Empire Delegation.

That conference, as we know, was never held. The Imperial War Cabinet never developed into an Imperial Peace Cabinet. Canada after the war reverted from the Borden policy to the Laurier policy. "Continuous consultation" ceased to be the rule after 1921, and the Borden-Smuts Commonwealth with a single united foreign policy distintegrated into the loose King-Hertzog British Entente of the 1920's in which the

[1] Sir Robert Borden, *Canadian Constitutional Studies*, p. 139.

six nations pursued each its own regional policy with only occasional meetings to discuss such common matters of interest as might crop up. This relationship in its turn broke down in the 1930's as Europe drifted towards another war and the distant Dominions slowly made up their minds that once again their common frontier was on the Rhine—or somewhere in Europe.

When the war came in September 1939, it resulted, as did the war of 1914, from a series of crises in which the real decisions had been almost entirely made by one government, His Majesty's Government in Great Britain, without effective consultation with the other governments. What, then, was the value of the new national status or the new method of conducting Commonwealth affairs which we were supposed to have achieved in the years 1914-19? Presumably the present Canadian government will frown upon a revival of the 1917 War Cabinet expedient. What other expedient then will the statesmen of our present war devise towards making united action more effective in the life and death European struggle to which they have again committed the Canadian people? In effect we are not much further forward than when Laurier and Borden were conducting their great argument as to Canada's position and responsibilities before 1914.

II. CANADA'S MILITARY EFFORT

In 1914 when war broke out Canada was one of the most completely unmilitary communities in the world. The Canadian militia consisted of (a) a Permanent Force of some 3,000 men, which had no system of reserves and found great difficulty in maintaining even this strength of 3,000 owing to the counter attractions of high wages in civil employment; (b) the non-permanent Active Militia with a strength of about 75,000 based upon a country-wide organization of Divisions or Districts, with militia units in each main town or city, and with a permanent staff acting under a Militia Council at Ottawa. Under the inspiration of official visits from Sir John French and Sir Ian Hamilton in the years just before 1914, a scheme of mobilization in the event of war had been worked out. But the militia, to tell the truth, was not taken very seriously by the country at large and hardly even by itself. It went through field-training each summer from twelve to sixteen days, but though men signed on for three years, the personnel of many units changed so thoroughly with each summer camp that training seldom reached beyond the most elementary stages. Officers and N.C.O.'s were many of them totally unqualified. In the 1913 training, on the eve of the great war, the Inspector-General noted the distressing fact that twenty-five per cent. of the officers were absent from training, half of these being absent without leave.

Things had been improving since Colonel Sam Hughes became Minister of Militia in 1911; or, at any rate, the expenditure of his department had increased from $7,000,000 in 1911 to $11,000,000 in 1914. But cynics were inclined to charge that the drill-halls which he was so fond of erecting in little Ontario towns had more to do with votes in the next election than with soldiers in the next war. When the war did break out the first action of the Minister was to scrap the scheme of mobilization which had been carefully prepared with the help of British experts and to improvise one of his own. Already, by the fall of 1914, his admirers were comparing him with Carnot, the organizer of victory; and he himself was confessing to ambitions of being not merely the Carnot but also the Napoleon of the Canadian armies. His speech to the first contingent as it left for Europe was said to be modelled upon General Bonaparte's famous address to the Army of Italy of 1796.[1]

It was out of such a background that the greatest communal achievement of the Canadian people in their history, the Canadian Corps of 1917-18, was brought about. Before that Christmas Eve of 1914 which was to inaugurate our celebration of a century of peace, Canada had sent overseas an expeditionary force of over 30,000 men, the largest armed force ever to cross the Atlantic up to that date, as Canadian newspapers, with their quick apprehension of significant historical events, were proud to point out. By the end of 1914, the government had enlisted some 91,000 men; by the end of 1915 this figure had grown to 215,000, and by October 1917, when conscription came into force, there had been recruited by voluntary enlistment 438,806 men.

The first Canadian division landed in France in February, 1915. By September there was a second division at the front, and in the winter of 1915-16 the third division came into existence. The fourth division arrived in time for the end of the Somme battles in October-November 1916. As at December 31, 1915, the Canadian forces in England amounted to 40,000

[1] *Borden Memoirs*, Vol. I, p. 465.

and in France to 52,000. By the end of 1916 these figures had grown to 131,000 in England and 109,000 in France. By the end of 1917 the figures were 110,000 in England and 141,000 in France.

Of the troops in France in 1917 and 1918 the Canadian Corps made up something over 100,000. In addition there were various other Canadian formations. There was the Canadian Railway Construction Corps, some 15,000 strong at the Armistice, who were in charge of most of the railway construction behind the British front lines; and the Canadian Forestry Corps, 24,000 strong by the time of the Armistice, some in England, some in France, who were supplying over seventy per cent. of the timber used by the Allied forces on the Western Front. One other great branch of the service whose work was mainly carried on outside the Corps was the Canadian Army Medical Corps. By the middle of 1917 its personnel amounted to over 14,000, and, in addition to the dressing stations, field ambulances and casualty clearing stations which were part of the Corps organization, it was conducting twenty hospitals in England and ten more overseas, mostly in France.

By 1918 the Canadians were also performing other odd jobs in various parts of the world. There was a bridging party of a few hundred experts sent from the Canadian Railway Troops to assist General Allenby in Palestine; and fifteen officers and twenty-seven N.C.O's formed part of the famous "Dunster Force" in Mesopotamia. In the latter part of the year, a brigade of Canadian Field Artillery was serving in Northern Russia against the Bolsheviks with Archangel as a base, and some smaller forces were at Murmansk; and another special Canadian force, some 4,000 strong, was in Vladivostock forming the bulk of the British contingent in Siberia.

In addition to all these, most spectacular of all the services manned by Canadians, was the Air Force. During the war over 8,000 Canadians held commissions in the Royal Flying Corps, the Royal Naval Air Service or, later, in the amalgamated Royal Air Force. The glorious record of Canadian flyers need not be emphasized here. By 1918 there were so many of them in the Royal Air Force and they were serving with such distinction that arrangements were made to establish a separate Canadian Air Force. The Armistice came before this separate force had gone into action in France.

In 1918 also there was organized a separate Canadian Tank Corps, one battalion of which was ready to cross to France at the time when the Armistice was signed.[1]

The Canadian Corps itself in 1917 and 1918 set up a record of continuous victory that was unsurpassed and indeed unequalled among all the troops on the Western front. "The Canadians", says Mr. Lloyd George in summing up his *War Memoirs*,[2] "played a part of such distinction [on the Somme in 1916] that thenceforward they were marked out as storm troops; for the remainder of the war they were brought along to head the assault in one great battle after another. Whenever the Germans found the Canadian Corps coming into the line they prepared for the worst".

[1] All these figures are from the *Report of the Ministry, Overseas Military Forces of Canada*, 1918.

[2] D. Lloyd George, *War Memoirs*, Vol. VI, p. 3367.

And everyone must agree that this tribute from the British prime minister was thoroughly well earned. The Canadians first showed their mettle when the troops of the 1st Division met the German gas attack at Ypres in May, 1915. Their heroic defence at Sanctuary Wood in June, 1916, followed by their brilliant series of attacks on the Somme from September to November, established their quality. In 1917 from Vimy in April to Hill 70 in August, to Passchendaele in October they had one long record of successful attacks in areas where all previous attacks by the allied forces had failed. Continuous co-operation with one another in winning battles, combined with the consciousness of being all Canadians, bred in them a strong *esprit de corps*. Unbroken success produced in all ranks an unquestioning confidence that no task could be set which they were not capable of accomplishing, and this confidence was justified to the full in the wonderful Hundred Days in 1918. On August 8— Ludendorff's "black day"—Canadians and Australians attacked side by side in front of Amiens and broke through the German lines for a seven-mile advance—the longest advance that any allied attack had achieved in the war up to this date. In the week beginning August 26 the Canadian Corps advancing from Arras broke the Drocourt-Quéant line, the strongest part of the German Hindenburg defence system. On September 27 they crossed the Canal du Nord in what Sir Arthur Currie considered the most brilliant manoeuvre of the war, and twelve days later captured Cambrai. And then in the last month of the war they conducted a triumphant fifty-mile advance ending up on Armistice Day at Mons on the very spot where the first British forces, the Old Contemptibles, had gone into action in August 1914.[1]

These actions cost heavy casualties. Infantry battalions had a wastage of ten per cent. of their strength per month during these years. The leaders of the Canadian Corps were not responsible for the strategy adopted by the Allied command who persisted from the spring of 1915 to the end of 1917 in large-scale frontal attacks upon the enemy along the Western front where he was most firmly entrenched. We know now that the two ablest and most dynamic men in the British government, Mr. Lloyd George and Mr. Churchill, as well as other members of the government such as Mr. Bonar Law, were from the start critical of or opposed to this strategy. The Easterners, so-called, wanted to use the mobility which was made possible by British sea power and to go around the flanks of the German western front by attacking in the Dardanelles, in the Balkans, through Palestine and Syria, on the Italian front against Austria, or at any point where Germany's weaker allies, Austria and Turkey, might be hit in a vulnerable spot. But the English and French high-command would not have it so. Their frontal attacks in France and Belgium cost the allies more men than they did the Germans and used up man power that might have achieved much greater results elsewhere, such great results in fact that the war, in the opinion at least of Mr. Lloyd George and Mr. Churchill, might have been shortened by a year or even two years. Mr. Lloyd George has a vivid phrase in which he denounces the "billy-goat"

[1] For a fuller account of the military operations of the Canadians see 'The Canadian Forces in the War', by F. H. Underhill, in Sir Charles Lucas (ed.) *The Empire at War*, Vol. II.

tactics of the western generals, in 1915, 1916, and 1917, as leading only to a succession of sickening thuds. It was these billy-goat tactics which consumed man-power at such a rate that by 1917 Canada was faced with the issue of conscription, because voluntary enlistment threatened to produce too few recruits to fill the gaps in the Corps at the front.

Let me turn, then, to the home front where the problem of reinforcements had to be met. Recruiting through 1914 and 1915 went on with easy success.[1] By 1916, when the country was committed to keeping up a Corps of four divisions in France, it was becoming somewhat more difficult. The government at the end of 1916 had set 500,000 enlistments as the figure at which to aim. In the first three months of that year, recruits streamed in at the rate of 1,000 a day; then they fell off to 800 a day for the next two months, and in the last half of the year the stream dwindled to 300 a day. In the early months of 1917 it threatened to become only a trickle. Recruiting campaigns became more strenuous. A National Service Board was set up to register and classify all males and find out how many really were available. But by this time the strain of the war was being felt acutely. The high cost of living was worrying all civilians. The political truce of 1914 between the two parties had been followed by bitter controversy. Scandal charges in connection with war contracts filled the air. And, worst of all, racial strife between Quebec and Ontario, starting over Regulation 17 of the Ontario Depart-

[1] The figures for enlistments, etc., and for the results of the 1917 election which are given here are taken from the volumes of the *Canadian Annual Review*, 1914-18.

ment of Education and continuing into a dispute about enlistment figures, had by 1917 reached a stage of almost unprecedented bitterness. Recruiting in the French province was handled with a stupidity so colossal and so persistent that one cannot help wondering whether it was only stupidity that led to all the mistakes or whether there was deliberate malignity at work as well in certain government circles.

The fact which stands out most clearly in an examination of enlistment figures is that enlistments were procured from different social groups in inverse proportion to the length of their connection with Canada. The British-born, who were in large number new arrivals, with a high proportion of males of military age, and who were also largely an urban population, supplied a far higher percentage of their total population than did the English-speaking Canadians born in Canada. And the French-Canadians, whose families had been settled longest of all in Canada and who had practically no ties with Europe, supplied the lowest percentage.

In the first contingent of 33,000 which sailed in October 1914, the British-born made up sixty-four per cent. Of the total voluntary enlistments up to October 1917, when conscription came into force, they formed forty-nine per cent. Official records do not classify the Canadian born into English-speaking and French-speaking, so that only approximate estimates of their relative enlistments are possible. But in 1917 the government announced that in that first contingent of 1914 there had been 1,217 French-Canadians, and that up to April 30, 1917, there had gone overseas 14,100 French-Canadians and 125,245 English-Canadians born in Canada.[1]

Sir Robert Borden returned from England in May, 1917, with the knowledge that the war was in a critical situation. The great French spring offensive in 1917 had failed disastrously. The spring of 1917 was the period in which submarine sinkings reached their height. Unfortunately, when he announced that the government had decided on conscription, the fires of racial bitterness had been fanned into a raging flame. Feelings of both races rose higher as they watched the long political crisis of that summer, marked by the passage of the *Military Service Act* and the *War Times Elections Act* and finally culminating in October, after months of intrigue and negotiations, in the Union government. By December, when the election came on, the campaign was fought amidst a crescendo of mutual racial recriminations and general hysteria.

The election returned a solid block of anti-conscription Liberals from Quebec with 62 out of the 65 seats. In the English provinces the majority for conscription was almost as decisive. Laurier's Liberals won only 20 seats in addition to these 62 in the whole of the rest of Canada. Altogether 115 Conservatives were returned with 38 Liberal-Unionists, giving the government 153 seats as against 82 for the opposition. In Ontario the Laurier Liberals won only 8 seats with 76 going to the government. In the Maritimes, where as usual passions were not quite so high as in the rest of Canada, the figures were 21 seats for the government

[1] Miss Elizabeth Armstrong in her book on *The Crisis of Quebec* 1914-18 estimates that some 15,000 French-Canadians served in France and that altogether there were 32-35,000 of them enlisted.

to 10 for the opposition. In the four western provinces, where voluntary recruiting had been most successful and where accordingly conscription feeling was strongest, the Liberals won only 2 seats as against 55 for the government. On the day after the election Quebec seemed to stand in almost complete political isolation.

Yet the figures for the ballots cast were by no means so overwhelming. Of the civilian vote the government candidates received 841,944; opposition candidates 749,849. The soldier vote as reported by the government officials was overwhelmingly for conscription—215,849 to 18,522. Most of the soldiers' ballots could be distributed among constituencies as the government saw fit, and they were shamelessly manipulated. Taking the vote as a whole as given, the anti-conscriptionists in the country and in the army were almost exactly three-quarters as many as the conscriptionists.

But when it came to calling up men under the *Military Service Act,* Quebec and Ontario did not show up so differently. Of 124,965 who were registered in Ontario in Class I, 116,092 claimed exemptions; of 115,602 registered in Quebec in Class I, 113,291 claimed exemptions. And the percentages of exemptions granted in the two provinces were not widely different. In numbers of defaulters among those finally called up, however, the picture was different. Quebec's percentage of defaulters was 41, Ontario's 9.

Conscription, as a matter of fact, did not produce the stream of recruits expected. By the spring of 1918, when the campaign opened on the Western Front, only 32,000 had been obtained, though Sir Robert Borden when he announced his policy in May, 1917, had spoken of 100,000 being needed. By November 11, 1918, there had been raised under the *Military Service Act* a total of 83,355 men of whom at that moment 7,100 were absent on compassionate leave, and 15,333 were absent on agricultural leave, giving a net product from a year's operation of the conscription law of 61,000 men. And most of these never reached France. Was this result worth all the controversy and bitterness which the issue caused in Canada?

Let me turn to another aspect of the national war effort which is pleasanter to contemplate—munitions supply.[1] When war broke out, Canada was almost as unequipped for the manufacture of shells and other munitions, as she was for other forms of military effort. With characteristic hustle, however, the Minister of Militia immediately formed a Shell Committee consisting of government officials and representatives of Canadian iron and steel manufacturers, and proceeded to seek orders from England. Before the end of 1914, 3,000 shells had actually been shipped overseas; in 1915 shell shipments were over five million. The Shell Committee, however, became involved in difficulties. Charges of patronage were made by the Opposition; the British government objected both to prices and to delays in delivery. In 1915 a British government mission, after long investigations in Canada, proposed to the Canadian government either that shell production be put directly under a Canadian Ministry of

[1] A full account of this side of Canada's war effort is given by Col. David Carnegie in his book, *The History of Munitions Supply in Canada,* 1914-18. My figures are taken from it.

Munitions as in England, or that an Imperial Munitions Board be set up to act directly under the British Munitions Ministry. The Borden government chose the latter alternative, and in November, 1915, the Imperial Munitions Board under the chairmanship of Sir Joseph Flavelle came into existence.

The story of its activities during the next three years surely forms the greatest romance in Canadian industrial history. Shell shipments rose in 1916 to twenty million and in 1917 to twenty-four million. These figures tell only part of the story because the shells shipped in later years included those of larger calibre and also the complete components of the shell —cases, fuses, explosives, everything. The most difficult part of shell manufacture was the production of fuses. To accomplish this the Imperial Munitions Board set up a national factory of its own in 1916 which was turning out fuses within five months after the site for the building was acquired. In 1917 it started to manufacture aeroplanes in another national factory. Other national factories produced high explosives and steel ingots. When the pressure for shipping became acute under German submarine attacks, the Board went into the building of ships. When the United States entered the war the Board proceeded to manufacture munitions for the Americans also. Altogether in these three years the Imperial Munitions Board spent 1250 million dollars of which 750 million were advanced by the Canadian government as a loan to the British government. Its annual expenditures in the last two years of the war were greater than those of the Canadian government itself. It had 675 factories working for it on one contract or another in 150 different towns in Canada. In 1917 between a quarter and a third of the shells fired from British guns on the Western front were made in Canada.

I must hasten to my conclusion.

What are we to say about our part in the first World War now that we are in the midst of the second one? Surely what emerges in starker outlines from those war years is what one observes everywhere traced less distinctly through the longer history of our years of peace, the strange dualism of Canadians: on the one hand their practical business capacity in handling concrete tasks with brilliant efficiency—the production of shells or the capture of German trenches—and on the other hand their persistent political incapacity in solving the more subtle intangible problems of learning to live together with one another in tolerant amity and concord. As to the general results of the war, it would be a painful and useless mockery today to ask what became of that better world for which we were fighting. But what became of all those Canadian soldiers who showed such indomitable courage, such individual initiative, such capacity for discipline and organization; what became of all those young captains and lieutenants and sergeants who led their men across no man's land, who cleared out trenches and captured pill-boxes; what became of them all in the post-war Canada to which they returned? How was it that their splendid qualities seemed to have no purpose but to be dissipated in the sorry futilities of the 1920's and 1930's? We are accustomed to speak of the nationhood which our country achieved as the result of its efforts in the war. Every four or five years our political leaders take us through an election campaign in which each party proclaims national unity and fresh national achievement as the result of its program. "With every change of Government", said Sir John Willison at the end of a long life, "Canada is made into a nation over again."[1] I feel an uneasy foreboding that thirty or fifty years from now some future historian, with a deeper bitterness and a deeper cynicism than that of Willison, will remark: "With every world war Canada is made into a nation over again."

[1] Sir John Willison, *Reminiscences, Political and Personal*, p. 308.

VI. CANADIAN EXTERNAL RELATIONS
by G. P. DE T. GLAZEBROOK

THREE comments by Canadians on external relations, made in time of crisis, may serve as some preface.

"We, the Mayor, the aldermen and citizens of Montreal, are gathered together in order . . . to assure Your Majesty of our personal affection and of our cordial and unanimous support at this critical time when the French and English nations are forced into a war against intolerance and despotism." (May 1854.)

"We are British subjects, and to-day we are face to face with the consequences which are involved in that proud fact. Long we have enjoyed the benefits of our British citizenship; to-day it is our duty to accept its responsibilities and its sacrifices.

The testimony of the ablest men . . . without dissenting voice, is that to-day the allied nations are fighting for freedom against oppression, for democracy against autocracy, for civilization against reversion to that state of barbarism in which the supreme law is the law of might." (Laurier in the House of Commons, August 19, 1914.)

"If parliament supports the administration this country will go into this war to defend its institutions and its liberties, and equally to be at the side of Britain, co-operating with her and with France towards those great and imperative ends." (Mackenzie King in the House of Commons, September 8, 1939.)

The voices of 1854, 1914, and 1939 are strikingly alike. It would be possible to find many more examples of the same view, and possible, too, to find passages expressing variant or even contradictory sentiments. No country has ever decided on a foreign policy with the approval of every one of its citizens. Foreign policy is the translation into action of the wishes, the beliefs, and the hopes of a majority—perhaps an overwhelming majority. The foreign policy of a country arises from its circumstances and position, its background and outlook; and, as Professor Martin said in the first lecture of this series, "it will be strange indeed if Canadian nationhood in world politics does not remain characteristically Canadian." The records of well over a century reveal the vital interest felt by our predecessors in the affairs of other countries, and of the meaning of those affairs to their own country. The debating clubs of the 1920's and 1930's could have repeated verbatim the arguments of a hundred years earlier—though they might have blushed before the vigour of expression and frankness of viewpoint of the past. Then, as in our day, it was fashionable to label people as "imperialists", "anti-imperialists", and so forth: the labels changing according to the phraseology of the time. "Collectivist", for instance, is a new label. This human weakness for simplification founders on the facts: in the 1840's tories became for a time "annexationists", and in the 1930's tory imperialists added the plume of "collectivist".

Some observers in the last two decades have found in the marked (though by no means new) divisions of opinion a phenomenon which they have believed to be peculiar to Canada. There come to one's mind such cleavages as that in the United States toward the War of 1812, that in France toward the war against Austria in 1859, or that in England with respect to the South African War. Whether or not it be held that Canada has seen more constant or stronger differences, the approach of the investigator will be best turned toward the explanation of these differences, the springs of these opinions. So to examine the problem is to reveal some at least of the complicated pattern of forces and circumstances, shifting and modifying as they may be, which are the causes both of doctrines and of actions.

The roots of Canadian civilization lie deeper than the history of Canada, for they are to be found in the soil of two old European states. First France, and then England, was the mother country of Canada, each contributing people, institutions, and culture. Such is the origin and the basic fact of the foreign relations of the Dominion. The two races have remained, never wholly fusing, and each finding a modified life in the conditions of the new world. The political severance of France and her colony by the Treaty of 1763 was given also a cultural side by the French revolution and its consequences. The French in Canada were thus almost altogether dissociated from their contemporaries in Europe, and yet remained different from their contemporaries in North America. While retaining their traditions of the eighteenth century, they were the most consciously Canadian element in the population, having no intimate ties either with Europe or with other American states.

While one link with Europe was cut, that with Great Britain remained, giving to Canada its unique rôle as the only colony in North or South America that did not become independent. It was in an empire, however, the rules of which were novel. At least by the twentieth century it could be said that imperial bonds were held in place only by the wish of those on whom the bonds were laid. In spite of the long discussions of imperial relations, and of the growingly independent power of the Dominion, it was never true that Canada was a nation struggling to be free. Rather it was a nation of people who were trying to decide, under ever different sets of circumstances, exactly what imperial relationship would best suit their own interests and point of view. Toward such decisions went a variety of considerations, selfish and unselfish, in proportions that can never be weighed. There were occasions when Canada sought more autonomy in some spheres without being able at once to achieve it; just as there were times when Great Britain would have been glad to lessen her responsibilities in a field in which Canadians needed support. Apart from delays of time, it was true that Canada's autonomy lay within her own reach.

Because of her constitutional position, Canada can more correctly be described as having an "external" policy than a "foreign" policy. The conduct of relations with foreign states has been complicated—whether it be considered in a particular case to have been helped or hindered—not only by the use of imperial machinery, but also by the special ties with imperial (as distinct from foreign) powers. The difference, however, between the position of Canada and that of an ordinary sovereign state, in respect of foreign policy, can be exaggerated. It is necessary in this, as in other cases, to attempt to analyze the factors from which the fundamental principles of external policy flow. Of these the imperial tie and the two races have been already touched on. To the latter should be added the increasing diversity of racial composition resulting from the heavy immigration of the twentieth century. In no event, nevertheless, is it safe to attempt a mathematical deduction from the origins of the people. The place in the Canadian economy played by foreign trade is a further factor of first importance, for on it depends the standard of living attained. The promotion of foreign trade, as far as governmental action is concerned, entails decisions on the Canadian tariff, and diplomatic negotiations with other states to secure favourable tariff adjustments on their part. It entails, too, the encouragement of transportation facilities by land and water: railways, canals, roads, harbours, navigation aids and shipping— and decisions on the use by foreign carriers of such of these as are Canadian. In so far as the external trade of Canada is by sea, the factor of defence plays a part in case of war.

The question of defence has also wider implications, and forms a main thread in the whole pattern of external relations. To define the most effective policy, strategic and political conditions must be assessed, and the action to be taken then be adjudged in relation to the capacity of the country. For several decades there has existed no problem of land defence, it being generally recognized that political relations with the only neighbouring state were such as to remove any prospect of war. The defence of the Atlantic and

Pacific coasts could not so lightly be dismissed. The consideration of the problem involved a characteristic mixture of political and strategic factors: the means of possible attack and the defence against it; and the probability and scale of that attack, together with the assistance that might be brought by other powers. Great Britain and the United States were the powers from which aid might, in certain cases, be anticipated. Defence, however, was not necessarily confined to Canadian territory. An undefined but well-understood principle has long existed that certain types of war or threat of war affecting Great Britain are of direct Canadian interest. Each case must be, and has been, decided on its merits. Frontier campaigns to the north of India or in the Soudan have, for example, been classed as outside the Canadian sphere; while Canadians fought in the Indian Mutiny and the South African War. The line of division proves on examination to have been a rough one determined by the threat of serious danger to the empire. Phrases about "imperialistic wars" (even if their meaning could be determined) have little relevance to the actual decisions.

The conduct of Canadian external policy and the constitutional development of the empire have been inter-related. Study of the latter has been full and penetrating, and has perhaps—because it has been more adequately treated—tended to conceal foreign policy, as distinct from the development of machinery related to it. It may be well, therefore, to attempt an examination of some aspects of the external relations of Canada in the period between the first and second great wars, as they have now come to be called. Our conclusions must be more than usually tentative for the evidence available is still very incomplete.

On the outbreak of war in 1914 the governmental machinery in Canada for the conduct of foreign policy was basically as it is to-day. The final authority was parliament, and there members of the government presented their proposals. Private members might ask questions, but in practice they infrequently took advantage of this privilege. The principal limitation of parliament's authority lay in the declaration of war, a prerogative retained by the King on the advice of his ministers in the United Kingdom. It did, however, lie entirely within the power of the Canadian parliament to decide whether the Dominion should participate in a war, and if so to what extent. The conduct of external relations—as distinct from decisions on policy—lay with the Department of External Affairs, set up in 1909. The office of secretary of state for external affairs was, by statute, held by the prime minister. The permanent head of the department was the under-secretary of state for external affairs. Three important modifications were made in this system at different dates after the war. First, correspondence between the British and Canadian governments passed through the direct channel, instead of the former indirect route by way of the governor-general and the colonial office. In the second place, beginning with the United States, Canada established legations in certain foreign states, and these sent ministers to Ottawa. Thirdly, Canada acquired the power to negotiate and conclude commercial treaties, without the assistance of a plenipotentiary from the United Kingdom.

The relations between the Dominion and the United Kingdom in the conduct of foreign policy have varied from time to time, but have always constituted a knotty problem. To invent a machinery which would provide for the implementing, as well as the discussion, of policy toward foreign states, and which would allow for co-operation without unacceptable commitments, seemed almost impossible. During and immediately after the War of 1914 a close co-operation through personal discussions seemed to be leading toward a solution, but before long it was clear that this expectation was not as yet to be realized. Apparently the ingenuity of even the British Empire had limits.[1]

Participation in the war of 1914-18 stimulated a new interest amongst the Canadian people in foreign affairs—or rather it increased an interest long existing and widened the circle of those to whom "foreign affairs" was more than a phrase. It had, in fact, much the same effect as on the peoples of other parts of the empire. With the sole exception of the Crimean War, which was far afield and limited in its effects on the civil population, the people of the United Kingdom had known nothing of major wars since those waged against Napoleon. English nurses threatened naughty children with the mere name of "Boney", but Canadians saw the American invaders burn the capital of Upper Canada. In the century between that world war and the next, the Civil War on this continent had been closer and more threatening to Canadians than were

[1] On this subject see W. K. Hancock, *Survey of British Commonwealth Affairs*, vol. 1 (Oxford, 1937); R. M. Dawson (ed.), *The Development of Dominion Status*, 1900-1936 (London and Toronto, 1937); A. G. Dewey, *The Dominions and Diplomacy: The Canadian Contribution* (2 vols., London, 1929).

the remote Black Sea campaigns to the English. While England spread its trade throughout the world, so, in a lesser degree, did Canada. The revolutions of 1848, the Crimean War, the Indian Mutiny, the Franco-Prussian War, and the Boer War were given generous space in Canadian newspapers. The Canadian government received frequent information from London on foreign affairs in the early twentieth century; and, if Sarajevo was a new name to the Canadian public, so it was in many another country; and the implications of the assassination were fully pointed out in the daily papers of Canadian cities.

The War of 1914 touched the Canadian people in the same way, though not perhaps to the same degree, as it did the people of Great Britain. They participated—with men, money, and munitions—to an extent hitherto unknown. Thus, before the war was over, Canadians were not only interested in world events; they were consciously playing a part in them. And the development of Canadian diplomacy, long under way, received an impetus that hurried it into a new stage. On October 27 Lloyd George cabled to Sir Robert Borden advising him to start for Europe without delay to discuss the projected peace conference with British delegates.[1] In reply Borden pointed out that Canada must be represented at the peace conference, a new departure which took some weeks to arrange owing to the opposition of other belligerents. In the meanwhile three of the Canadian plenipotentiaries (as they became), Borden, Foster, and Sifton, sailed for England. During the preliminary discussions in London, and later at Paris, the Canadian representatives played an active

[1] Canadian *Sessional Papers*, 41 J, 1919.

part. Up to a point the matters under discussion were not of direct interest to Canada. The Canadian representatives were on various committees. Borden, for example, was vice-chairman of the committee dealing with Greek affairs, which appeared to be far removed from the Canadian sphere, although they had a sequel later at Chanaq. On several occasions Borden expressed views on the future of the German colonies. Canada, he stated more than once, was opposed to territorial aggrandizement. This he saw not only as a proper principle in itself but one that fitted in with the general Canadian aim of good relations with the United States. "I expressed the opinion that one of the most important assets to be gained from the war would be assured goodwill and clear understanding between Great Britain and the United States. There were very strong elements, such as the German and Irish, in the United States which were bitterly opposed to the Empire and these must not be given a plausible argument that we had gone into the war for territorial aggrandizement."[1] He did, however, support the claims of other Dominions to retain German colonies, but only in so far as these were necessary for the safety of the empire, and on condition that they be held as mandates. Lloyd George records that he had sounded Borden on the project of Canada assuming the administration of the British West Indies on behalf of the Empire, but he "found that Sir Robert Borden was deeply imbued with the American prejudice against the government of extraneous possessions and peoples which did not

[1] H. Borden (ed.), *Robert Laird Borden: His Memoirs* (2 vols., Toronto, 1938), 884.

form an integral part of their own Union", and the subject was dropped.[1] Time and again Borden stressed his point that efforts should be made to use the conference as a means of closer understanding between the United States and the British Empire. A member of the American House Commission, and an enthusiast for that cause, George Louis Beer, suggested unofficially that Canada might acquire the Alaska panhandle in exchange for territory in the Caribbean—the object being to avoid friction over the former.[2] It is known that Borden discussed Alaska with Lord Milner,[3] but there the record ends.

Relations with Russia came up both before and at the conference. At the imperial war cabinet, and again at the inter-allied conference in December, Borden expressed the opinion that the allies should "induce the governments of the various states in Russia to send representatives to Paris."[4] To the British Empire delegation he suggested the desirability of getting in touch with the Bolshevik government.[5] But whatever else might be done, Canada would not send an army to Russia.[6]

Two other questions of immediate concern to Canada came before the conference. The first was the proposal to create a commission or commissions to regulate international traffic by land, water, and air. The Canadians refused to consider the idea of a European

[1] D. Lloyd George, *The Truth About the Peace Treaties* (2 vols., London, 1938), 554.

[2] Borden, *op. cit.*, 907.

[3] *Ibid.*, 909.

[4] Lloyd George, *op. cit.*, 199, 322.

[5] *Ibid.*, 348.

[6] *Ibid.*, 346.

commission controlling railway and canal transport between their own country and the United States. On the question of air traffic they pointed to the four thousand miles of unguarded frontier, and the exceptional relations arising out of it—relations which could not be fitted into the straitjacket of European rules. The second question was the Japanese demand that the Covenant of the League of Nations should contain an endorsement of the principle of racial equality. To this Borden proposed an alternative formula endorsing the "principle of equality between nations and just treatment of their nationals."[1] He was also outspoken against draft clauses for the International Labour Organization which would have interfered with Canadian restrictions on oriental labour, and "might lead to great disorder, possibly rebellion on the Pacific Coast of the United States and of Canada."[2]

Just as the Canadian government had insisted on separate representation at the peace conference, so its representatives there had to wage a further struggle—principally against the United States delegation—for separate membership in the League of Nations and the International Labour Organization, and for the right to be elected to the council of the former and the governing body of the latter. Taking, as they did, a part in the formulation of these two organizations, the Canadian delegates were fully aware that membership involved obligations as well as honour and authority; and they used what influence they could command to have the terms drawn agreeable to their own policy. The implications of the Labour Convention

[1] Borden, *op. cit.*, 927.
[2] *Ibid.*, 933.

for Canadian immigration rules have already been mentioned. In connection with the implementing of agreements made in the International Labour Organization the question arose as to the constitutional position of federal states. On being asked about this by the British delegation, Borden referred the question to Doherty, the minister of justice, whose opinion was that Art. 132 of the British North America Act, which gave to the Canadian parliament the powers necessary for carrying out obligations arising out of treaties, would cover the point.[1] The commitments created by the League Covenant were also carefully studied. In March 1919 Borden attempted, though without success, to have Article 10 deleted from the draft, believing that it bound the member states to participate in possible military action in any part of the world.

Canadian statesmen were, like those of other countries, seeking to bend world conditions as near as might be to the needs and advantages of their own circumstances. The most fundamental of the factors affecting Canada was its dual rôle as an American and a world power. On the one hand, was a relatively secure position on the American continent and favourable political and economic relations with the United States. On the other, were Canada's position in the British Empire and her wider trading connections with that empire and with foreign states. A pull in both directions had long existed, but the balance had frequently changed. A main objective of Canadian foreign policy has been to maintain a workable com-

[1] J. T. Shotwell (ed.), *The Origins of the International Organization* (2 vols., New York, 1934), i, 155.

promise between the extremes of complete American-
ism and detachment from America. On this continent
the Canadian orbit, with the exception of some
business interests, stops at the Rio Grande. Toward
South America Canada has always remained aloof
and there has been little indication of a desire to join
the Pan-American Union. It is less easy to find the
eastern Canadian frontier. At times on the Rhine, it
advances and recedes according to changing circumstances. Once it was stretched to Vladivostock, but
later was not allowed to reach the shorter distance to
Asia Minor. In a world of five powers, Bismarck
concluded, one should be *à trois*. Canada's world was of
three powers and in this too she aimed to be *à trois*.
The bogey of Canadian policy, ever since the fear of
American aggression was removed, has been a break
between the United Kingdom and the United States
severe enough to force a decision to remain with the
one, and so to lose the other, friend.

Such was the danger as it appeared to the Canadian
government in 1921. It was understood that the
Anglo-Japanese alliance would terminate in that year
unless it were renewed. Since 1902, when it had first
been signed, the alliance had been of benefit to both
parties. Renewed in 1911 in a modified form, it had
contained a clause saving any obligation on Great
Britain to support Japan in a war against the United
States, and Canada had approved of its continuance.
But the expansionist policy of the Japanese governments during and after the War of 1914 caused alarm
on the part of the powers interested in the Far East,
and materially widened the cleavage between Japan
and the United States.

In February 1921 the Canadian government presented to the British government an argument against
renewal of the treaty, and recommended a conference,
to include Japan and the United States, on Pacific
affairs.[1] The Canadian position was taken mainly
because of the view that American hostility to the
treaty was sufficient seriously to threaten Anglo-
American friendship, so essential to Canadian and
English interests. There was talk of a war between
the United States and Japan, and if that should break
out American relations with Britain would be further
strained. It was even possible that Canadian neutrality might be endangered by military and naval operations on the west coast. A far happier arrangement
than the old treaty would be a multilateral agreement
on Far Eastern affairs.

Other parts of the Empire saw the issue differently.
Australia and New Zealand, far from America and
close to the East, believed that safety was better
secured by alliance with Japan than by any other
method. In Great Britain it was recognized that the
alliance had been of value in the past, and it was
felt that its continuance might well be a protection
against revived German or Russian power, as well as
a basis for agreement on commercial interests in Japan,
and even more in China. It was, however, an axiom
of British policy that good relations with the United
States must be maintained. Were American objections
to the treaty so great that it must be abandoned?
Or was there not a possible compromise?

It happened that the Imperial Conference met in
June 1921, at just the time that a decision on this

---

[1] *Canadian Annual Review,* 1921, 102.

major question of foreign policy affecting both the Dominions and the United Kingdom had to be made. In the history of imperial foreign policy there is no parallel to that conference. It followed closely on the precedents of joint policy in the later part of the war and at the peace conference, but it stands alone as a personal discussion of, and decision on, a major aspect of foreign policy. Other matters were also debated at length, but the most important issue was the alliance. It seems clear that by the time the conference met the British cabinet had agreed on a renewal of the treaty, though modified to meet the conditions of the Covenant of the League, and perhaps to placate American opinion.[1] In the early stages of the conference it was assumed that the alliance would terminate in July and that a decision had to be reached quickly. Hughes and Massey urged renewal strongly, and it was left to Meighen to argue the case against it. By all those who took part in the discussions it was taken for granted that the issue was an imperial one, though the representatives of each government had special interests to consider; and an honest attempt was made to evaluate all the considerations. Mr. Meighen's first concern was to represent the strength of American opposition to the treaty, and it seems to have been his forceful advocacy, combined with a growing uncertainty on the part of the British government that they could appease American opposition by any other means, that led Lloyd George and his colleagues to explore the possibilities of a multilateral treaty. Conversations with the governments concerned were carried on by the foreign secretary; and at the same time a revised interpretation of the position of the treaty was reached, by which it would not expire without a year's notice. That saving elasticity of time allowed for a conference of the Pacific powers before any final decision was made on the treaty. The negotiations for a conference bore fruit in an invitation issued early in July by the United States government to a conference in Washington; and an understanding was reached in London that if the Washington meeting was a success the alliance would be dropped.[1]

The case of the debate on the alliance has frequently been cited to illustrate the potential influence of Canada on imperial policy. Here was no isolationism, but a vigorous thrust into international affairs. It must be remembered, however, that the case is an unusual one. At least three Dominions as well as the United Kingdom were vitally interested in it. Each believed that its political and strategic position was involved, and that a false decision might have serious consequences on it. The debate at the Imperial Conference was not a duel between the Canadian and United Kingdom representatives: nor was it that the Canadian representative used arguments that were new to the British cabinet. It was a problem of balancing the factors, of choosing between risks. The Australian and Canadian policies were both consistent throughout, and in the end the Canadian view prevailed.

In November the scene shifted to Washington. In spite of an early difficulty arising out of the failure

---

[1] W. M. Hughes, *The Splendid Adventure* (Toronto, n.d.), 131.

of the American government to invite the Dominions, they were in the end represented in the same manner as at the peace conference. During the conference at Washington, though not strictly as a part of it,[1] the four naval powers in the Pacific—the United States, the British Empire, France and Japan—signed the Four Power Treaty, "for the preservation of the general peace and the maintenance of their rights in the region of the Pacific Ocean." The treaty was not an alliance. It was merely an agreement by each party to respect the others' rights, and to confer on any dispute concerning those rights. On the ratification of the treaty, the Anglo-Japanese Treaty was to terminate. It was signed by the representatives of the dominions.

The Near Eastern crisis of 1922 had for Canada a very different meaning from the Far Eastern question of a year earlier, for the first bore directly on Canadian interests and the second did not. In 1922 no opportunity existed for a round-table discussion. If it had, the sudden request to Ottawa for support could have been avoided, the virtual refusal of which did nothing to smooth the imperial way. Had there been such preliminary discussion it is a fairly safe speculation that the Dominion government would have sought to escape any responsibility, regarding the issue as outside its orbit. In the form that it took, the Chanaq incident demonstrated both the limitations of Canadian interests abroad, and the still imperfect state of the machinery for imperial co-operation, or even for

---

[1] *Conference on the limitation of armaments held at Washington November 12, 1921 to February 6, 1922: report of the Canadian delegate* (Canadian *Sessional Papers*, 47, 1922).

imperial understanding. Happily the threatened war between Turkey and Great Britain was avoided. If it had broken out the Canadian government and parliament would have been forced to decide, as they had many times before had to decide, whether this particular cause should lead to Canadian participation. That there might have been a difference of opinion on the point is shown by the caution of the government on the one hand, and the large number of voluntary offers of military service on the other.

Separate membership in the League of Nations was insisted on by the Canadian government, and the demand for the right to be elected to the council further demonstrated that Canada's position in the League was to be in no way subordinate to that of sovereign states. For a time at least the public interest in this constitutional development tended to over-shadow the commitments that were bound up in membership. But the governments of the day were fully conscious of the need for adjudging obligations; and, as in all other states, they attempted to strike a balance between the advantages that it was hoped to gain through the League and the actions to which they might be committed. The essence of the Covenant was its provision for collective security against aggression by means of a universal guarantee to each member. For a member of the British Empire this was the old issue in a new form. In that smaller circle, tied by tradition and common blood, Canada had not bound herself to automatic sanctions against an aggressor, but had preferred to leave each case for decision on its own merits. How could she go so much further in this greatly widened circle? When the

Covenant was being drafted in 1919 Sir Robert Borden attempted to have Article 10 either omitted or drastically modified. Failing in that, the Canadian delegation moved in the first assembly that the article be struck out. That motion too fell by the wayside, and the Canadians then—in the fourth assembly—proposed an interpretative resolution which read in part as follows:

It is in conformity with the spirit of Article 10 that, in the event of the Council considering it to be its duty to recommend the application of military measures in consequence of an aggression or danger or threat of aggression, the Council shall be bound to take into account, more particularly, of the geographical situation and of the special conditions of each state.

The last phrase was full of meaning to other states as well as to Canada. Some were, in the jargon of the day, "nervous states" or "consumers of security". To Poland or to Belgium, to Albania or Greece—to these and other states fearful that the *status quo* of 1919 might be upset—Article 10 was the only solid guarantee in a dangerous world. The French never made any secret of their opinion that the Covenant was so watered down that it could not be regarded as sufficient protection: so strongly did they feel this that the additional Anglo-American treaties of guarantee had to be constructed to fill the breach. Hardly a boundary in continental Europe was untouched by the settlement of 1919, and it is not surprising that those states which had gained by the treaties, or even owed their very existence to them, should look to them for protection. If anything had been needed to confirm them in their views it would have been the sympathy expressed by the losers—Austria, Bulgaria, and Hungary—for the Canadian assault on Article 10.

The refusal of the American senate to ratify the treaties deprived the League of the support of the great power originally most insistent on its creation. To Canada that decision had a further significance. For North America as a whole to be involved in the affairs of Europe in every time of crisis spelt a new responsibility: but for Canada, a small power, to represent North America alone was a far graver position. Canada, Dandurand told the assembly in 1925, would be loyal to the Covenant. But, he went on, "we are not forgetful of the conditions under which we signed it. Canada was then far from thinking that she would have the whole burden of representing North America when appeals would come to our continent for assistance in maintaining peace in Europe."[1] And there was a further implication of serious moment: that Canada would find Great Britain and the United States following different, and even conflicting, policies, the one in the League and the other outside it. The probable cause of divergence lay in the Far East, the only area in which the two powers were, generally speaking, equally active, and where the writ of the Monroe Doctrine did not run. Such a crisis was, as we have seen, narrowly avoided in 1921.

During the twenties there continued the pull between the demand for security and the resistance to the commitments by which it might be obtained: or between the consumers and the producers of security.

[1] Quoted in C. A. W. Manning, *Policies of the British Dominions in the League of Nations* (Oxford, 1932), 58.

Two plans intended to provide for security and disarmament on a universal basis were introduced into the assembly of the League: the Draft Treaty of Mutual Assistance and the Geneva Protocol for the Peaceful Settlement of International Disputes. Both were referred after debate to the states members of the League, and both were rejected by the United Kingdom and the Dominions. The Canadian government's reply to the first proposal was summed up in the remark that "so far as it purports to impose a future obligation to take specific action in circumstances incapable of present definition, it would be hopeless to expect the people of Canada to accept it."[1] When the Protocol came before the recently elected conservative British government late in 1924 that government proposed to the Dominions a special meeting of the Imperial Conference in the following March, so that, as the prime minister said, the empire should have a single policy, determined after personal consultation. It proved impossible to arrange such a meeting, and correspondence was therefore the only method of discussion. There does not, however, seem to have been any difference of opinion. On March 4 cables between London and Ottawa crossed. The colonial secretary's despatch was a notification that the cabinet had come to the conclusion that they could neither accept themselves, nor recommend that the Dominions should accept, the Protocol. The Canadian government's decision was that the Protocol was not in the interests either of Canada or the League. They objected particularly to "its rigid

[1] Quoted in R. A. Mackay and E. B. Rogers, *Canada looks abroad* (London and Toronto, 1938), 328.

provisions for application of economic and military sanctions in every future war", and gave as one ground for their decision "the effect of non-participation of the United States upon attempts to enforce sanctions and particularly so in the case of contiguous countries like Canada".[1]

In the Locarno agreements of 1925 Europe turned from universal to regional guarantees of security, and Canada was consequently not a party. Locarno and the admission of Germany into the League gave a better complexion to international affairs. The lessening of strain in that field was accompanied by rising prosperity; and for a few brief years Canadians were able to think of external relations more in terms of mounting foreign trade than of political commitments and guarantees. In 1926 the total of foreign trade showed a considerable increase over the previous four years, and in 1929 it reached an all-time high. In Canada, as in other countries in the dozen years after the war, the absence of any danger of further large-scale hostilities in the near future, combined with the hope of collective security and disarmament, led to a lack of stress on military or naval preparations during the twenties. In the early thirties expectations of an agreement for general reductions arising out of the Disarmament Conference, added to financial problems of the depression, still kept Canadian military expenditures low.

All too soon came the descent from the national and international bliss of the late twenties. The dramatic beginning of the depression in New York

---

[1] *Protocol for the peaceful settlement of international disputes: correspondence relating to the position of the Dominions* (Cmd. 2458, 1925).

in 1929 was followed by declining international trade until, in 1933, the external trade of Canada was but a third of what it had been in 1929. Political events were no less upsetting. The invasion of Manchuria in 1931 and the National Socialist revolution in Germany in 1933 heralded long-drawn-out crises in the two parts of the world in which Canada had shown most interest in the past. The problem of saving, or even modifying, the settlement of 1919 was replaced by the problem of saving international peace. The post-war era had become the pre-war era.

In the particular crises of the thirties Canadian policy followed traditional lines. While the answer to be given by the League in respect to Japan's actions in China was discussed in the assembly, one of the Canadian delegates so balanced the arguments and stressed conciliation as to give an impression of seeking to avoid the issue of sanctions against a state that was commonly regarded as having committed an act of aggression. But, apart from this preliminary caution, the Canadian representatives accepted the decision of the assembly against Japan. The course of events in the Italo-Ethiopian War was similar. Some alarm was felt in this country when a Canadian member of the Committee of Eighteen suggested that sanctions should be extended to cover oil and coal, and when this seemed to place Canada in the van of the countries hovering on the narrow margin between economic sanctions and war. The suggestion was explained in Canada as a personal opinion, and it was stated by the secretary of state for external affairs that the government was not taking the initiative in extending the list.

Canadian experience in foreign affairs, as illustrated by the cases referred to, had been considerable in the two decades after 1919. Canada has, of course, at no time played a leading part in international politics. Small powers seldom do, and especially is this true of a country whose interests are conservative; which wishes to conserve the *status quo*. But a foreign policy which appears at times to be essentially negative may be as truly a foreign policy as that pursued by a state whose circumstances demand action and change.

For the post-1919 years, and for many years before, there may be found a vein of consistency in Canadian foreign relations, the basis of which is in some respects strikingly similar to that of Great Britain. There is the same desire for a peaceful world coloured as far as possible by generally liberal principles, a world in which international trade may flourish, and in which the burden of defence is cut to the minimum. Canada, like England, has fought shy of alliances and commitments in so far as national safety has allowed it. Like the English, we have been shy of crusades, of ideologies, and of inexorable logic. Canadians, too, have encouraged compromise, pursued peace—perhaps not always in the wisest way, but by any road which seemed open. We have been opportunists, hoping for the best, not always preparing for the worst. We have been reluctant to nip dangerous moves in the bud, thinking, perhaps, that the danger might never flower.

Isolationism is not a policy peculiar to the Americas. It is hardly more than a generation since England reluctantly left her "splendid isolation" so comfortably cherished in the late nineteenth century. And so with Canada: the South African War, the War of 1914, the War of 1939 all attest that there are causes for which Canada will take up the sword. Chanaq and Locarno show that there have been also cases regarded as outside the Canadian sphere. It is no part of this lecture to attempt to define the causes of this present war, far less to assess the elements of altruism or national interest, of sentiment or logic. It is but a study of some of the forces behind Canadian external policy, some cases in which that policy has operated, and a suggestion that Canadians —living in what has been known as a "new country" for 335 years—have not been altogether oblivious of the outside world and of their relations to it—in peace or in war.

VII. CANADIAN AND IMPERIAL WAR CABINETS

by R. MacGregor Dawson

PARLIAMENTARY government as it is known and practised in Great Britain and the Dominions has had a most interesting history, and no part of it, perhaps, has exceeded in significance that of the past twenty-five years. This has been particularly true of the central pillar of these governments, the cabinet itself, which has been subjected to a number of critical tests during this period. One of these tests stands out above all others, the strain imposed on the cabinet system during the last war—an ordeal which is unhappily being repeated at the present time. Crises inevitably bring an enormous pressure on the executive branch of government; it is the part which must bear the brunt of an emergency and which is most likely to be twisted and distorted by the stress of unusual and stirring events. At the outset of the last war, adjustments in the administration were made slowly and reluctantly, but when the seriousness of the situation became manifest the cabinet, particularly in Great Britain, showed an astonishing capacity to make extensive changes which profoundly altered its structure and greatly increased the effectiveness of the national effort. This elasticity was again evident with the return of peace; for the cabinet was able with little apparent difficulty to resume substantially its old form and place in the government, and treat the war as a mere incident in what had already been a most eventful life. It is the task of this essay to examine briefly the ways in which the British, Canadian, and Imperial cabinets in the past war succeeded in working out new forms of cabinet organization, the extent to which these devices were continued after the peace, and the attempts which are being made to solve similar problems in these countries today.

In the early part of the last war all important commitments affecting Empire affairs were made by the British Cabinet. The great bulk of the decisions, however, were usually taken, at least in the first instance, by a much smaller body, the name and composition of which varied as the war progressed. At first, the Prime Minister and the heads of the fighting departments were responsible for the day-to-day operations, and the Committee of Imperial Defence, a pre-war body with an elastic personnel and known at this time as the War Council, was consulted on new or more general operations. Within three months of the outbreak of hostilities Mr. Asquith decided to substitute for these two groups a Cabinet Committee of six or seven of the most important members, together with Mr. Balfour from the Opposition and certain experts who attended permanently or on special occasions. The proceedings of this body were copied from those of the old Committee of Imperial Defence, and it kept records of its decisions which were in due course forwarded to the departments concerned. The Cabinet retained, of course, its pre-eminent position, all important matters were referred to it, and it could and at times did assert its ultimate authority.[1]

In 1915 after the first Coalition Government was formed, the conduct of the war passed into the hands of what was called the Dardanelles Committee, a group of eleven Ministers reinforced by a number of experts. Its size and the divergent political views and personalities of its members made it a most ineffective and cumbersome instrument. "It was much too large," writes Asquith's biographer, "it was highly argumentative, and when it had finished its debates, the Cabinet, as often as not, claimed the right of debating its conclusions all over again from the beginning, with results that were negative or mischievous."[2] After a few months' experience, Asquith proposed that the Committee, which had gradually acquired control over all war activity and had been re-named in consequence the War Council, should be abolished, and that two small bodies, one on the actual conduct of the war, the other on finance, should be appointed; but the suggestion evoked no enthusiasm in any quarter.[3] Finally, in November, 1915, the Cabinet itself reluctantly decided that the management of the war must be placed under the control of a smaller executive, and a War Committee whose numbers ranged from five to eight was appointed. But once again the result was disappointing. The Committee found itself spending too

[1] Lord Oxford and Asquith, *Memories and Reflections*, Vol. II, pp. 104-5. J. A. Spender and C. Asquith, *Life of Lord Oxford and Asquith*, Vol. II, pp. 126-9.

[2] *Ibid.*, vol. II, p. 186, cf. p. 180. W. S. Churchill, *The World Crisis*, Vol. II, pp. 401-2, 412.

[3] J. A. Spender and C. Asquith, *Life of Lord Oxford and Asquith*, Vol. II, pp. 186-7.

much time and energy on domestic matters which, while connected with the war, were not intimately bound up with it. Its meetings tended, through consultation with other Ministers, to become far too large, and these provoked as a consequence exactly the kind of discussion which the Committee was supposed to avoid. Moreover, the appeal to the Cabinet was always available, and its authority and responsibility were frequently invoked when any controversial topic was under consideration.[1] Unhappily such appeals frequently served but to prolong the dispute and postpone the settlement. For the Cabinet was cursed with hesitation and indecision: it contained too many powerful and uncongenial personalities; the questions pressing for solution were complex and many-sided; the organization of the Cabinet's work was faulty; and the Prime Minister, Mr. Asquith, had gradually lost the confidence of many of his associates.[2] The result was dramatic and decisive. In December, 1916, Mr. Lloyd George, exasperated by the Cabinet's general infirmity of purpose and by the delay and uncertainty of the Prime Minister, demanded certain changes in the composition and organization of the directing committee. These Mr. Asquith refused to accept; and the ensuing crisis forced his retirement and the appointment of Mr. Lloyd George in his stead.

The first act of Mr. Lloyd George was the establishment of an entirely new kind of executive body, one

[1] Lord Crewe, in Lord Oxford and Asquith, *Memories and Reflections,* Vol. II, pp. 152-4.

[2] D. Lloyd George, *War Memoirs,* Vol. II, pp. 973-8. W. I. Jennings, *Cabinet Government,* pp. 228-35.

which was quite without parallel in British constitutional history. Previous Cabinets had been composed almost entirely of Ministers at the head of the great administrative departments, such as Foreign Affairs, the Treasury, the Admiralty, and the Home Office; but all the members of this new Cabinet were without portfolios and had no departmental work of any kind, except Mr. Bonar Law, who was both Chanceller of the Exchequer and Leader of the House of Commons. A further change was made by reducing the size of the Cabinet from twenty-three to five, although later this was on occasion increased to six and seven. Thus at a single stroke Mr. Lloyd George had created a small working executive, whose members were released from the routine of departmental duties and were consequently free to devote their entire efforts to the major problems of war. Even the Prime Minister, while he might frequently attend the sittings of the House, could come and go as he pleased without giving to Parliament the time and constant attention which the task of leadership normally demanded. The War Cabinet was thus able to remain in almost continuous session without disturbing materially the administration of any of the departments;[1] its limited membership facilitated discussion and discouraged debate; it was fully competent to make rapid decisions through its position as the general coordinating authority of all government activities. The old Cabinets, said Mr. Lloyd George in his explanation

[1] The preceding Cabinet and its War Committee held 59 meetings in 146 days; the War Cabinet in the same length of time held 146 meetings. In eighteen months the War Cabinet held 555 meetings in 474 working days, excluding Sundays. Lord Curzon in *British House of Lords Debates*, June 19, 1918, p. 267.

to the House, were peace structures, "they were organized for a different purpose and a different condition of things. The kind of craft you have for river or canal traffic is not exactly the kind of vessel you construct for the high seas. . . . But a Cabinet of twenty-three is rather top-heavy for a gale. I do not say that this particular craft is best adapted for Parliamentary navigation, but I am convinced it is the best for the War, in which you want quick decision above everything. Look at the last two years. . . . We are all perfectly certain . . . that the Allies have suffered disaster after disaster through tardiness of decision and action. . . . It is true that in a multitude of counsellors there is wisdom. That was written for Oriental countries in peace times. You cannot run a war with a Sanhedrim."[1]

This War Cabinet, moreover, was the real power in the government and not merely a committee of a superior body which kept it under surveillance and control. It consulted with Ministers and officials, it deliberated for the most part in camera, it made all decisions of vital consequence. Ministers thus became simply heads of the administrative departments who gave advice and did as they were instructed; and they naturally accepted no responsibility whatever for Cabinet decisions. They were summoned to attend the meetings of the Cabinet when matters concerning their departments were under consideration; they brought their experts with them; and the latter were considered to be completely free to dissent from their ministerial superiors and express their own views without reserve. "This opening of the doors of the

[1] *British House of Commons Debates*, Dec. 19, 1916, pp. 1333-4.

Cabinet room," said Lord Curzon, "is, of course, an entirely new feature in our system. . . . In the olden days the Cabinet was regarded as almost sacrosanct. It was a kind of Star Chamber which sat with closed doors, through which no one was allowed to penetrate, and across whose threshold the shadow of a stranger was only on the rarest occasions allowed to fall. Today if we are discussing questions affecting labour, shipping, agriculture, or the Irish question, outside authorities are freely admitted. The Cabinet benefits in my judgment from that, because we hear the views of the experts expressed from their own lips, and the experts themselves are grateful for this system because they have a chance of being heard. They hear the discussion in the War Cabinet and they are made acquainted with the decision that is arrived at."[1]

Lord Curzon's account points to another radical innovation in cabinet practice which was also begun at this time, namely, the lifting of the curtain of secrecy and mystery which had previously hung about all its deliberations. The Cabinet meetings had always been secret, there had never been any formal order of business, no minutes had been kept, and only the Prime Minister was allowed to take a few furtive notes in order to give the King an accurate account of the proceedings. The disadvantages of this informality are obvious; for on frequent occasions Ministers were uncertain as to the exact terms of the decision which

[1] *British House of Lords Debates,* June 19, 1918, pp. 270-1. From December 9th, 1916, to December, 1917, no less than 248 persons other than members of the War Cabinet and the Secretariat attended its meetings. The War Cabinet, Report for the Year 1917, *Parl. Pap. (Great Britain)* 1918, Cd. 9005, p. 2.

had been made, or, indeed, if any decision had been reached at all. The following letter, written by Lord Hartington's private secretary to the private secretary of Mr. Gladstone in 1882, furnishes a good illustration of ministerial embarrassment arising from this cause.

My dear Eddy,

Harcourt and Chamberlain have both been here this morning and *at* my chief about yesterday's Cabinet proceedings. They cannot agree about what occurred. There must have been some decision, as Bright's resignation shows. My chief has told me to ask you what the devil *was* decided, for he'll be damned if he knows. Will you ask Mr. G. (that is Mr. Gladstone) in more conventional and less pungent terms?[1]

Both the secrecy and the informality of Cabinet procedure were affected by Mr. Lloyd George's reforms. The Cabinet still continued to deliberate in secret; but the admission of other people to its councils, as noted above, as well as the presence of its own secretaries made substantial inroads on this custom. One precedent established by the old Committee of Imperial Defence and succeeding War Committee was now carried over to the War Cabinet itself, when it was given a secretariat charged with the duty of setting up and maintaining a more business-like procedure. From this time the Cabinet met at regular intervals; it received daily reports from the fighting services; it canvassed the foreign or diplomatic situation at each session; it went systematically through special agenda prepared by its own staff; its discussions and decisions were carefully recorded day by day. The topics to be

[1] *British House of Lords Debates*, Dec. 21, 1932, p. 529. Cf. *ibid.*, pp. 519-35.

considered at each sitting were linked up with a time-table, and the Ministers and others concerned were informed of the hour when the subjects which affected their special field would arise for discussion. Every effort was made to secure prompt attention and action on current problems, and the Cabinet usually succeeded in cleaning up its routine programme for the week in the first two or three days. As soon as a decision was taken, a copy of the Minute was sent to each department affected so that both Minister and officials would be fully informed. Moreover, the Secretary kept in constant touch with all the departments, and he reported to the Cabinet the action which had been taken in response to its orders. An immense amount of work was transacted by delegation. Matters were referred as they arose to individual members of the War Cabinet, to committees of Ministers, or to others, and they were either given power of decision or were required to investigate and report back to the War Cabinet itself.[1]

An incidental advantage of the new scheme was that it allowed the number of administrative departments to be expanded almost indefinitely without increasing the size of the Cabinet itself. The Ministries of Shipping, Labour, Food, and Pensions were soon formed, and to these were later added Reconstruction, National Service, and Air. A more dubious innovation was to place business men instead of experienced parliamentarians in charge of some of these departments, on the theory that such hard-headed men of

[1] The War Cabinet, Report for the Year 1917, *Parl. Pap. (Great Britain)*, 1918, Cd. 9005, pp. 1-4. *British House of Lords Debates*, June 19, 1918, pp. 265-82. D. Lloyd George, *War Memoirs*, Vol. III, pp. 1080-2. W. I. Jennings, *Cabinet Government*, pp. 186-93, 208-16.

affairs would be best fitted to deal with practical
matters. A shipping owner, an oil magnate, a wholesale grocer, a newspaper director, a mine operator, and
others with similar qualifications, were thus given
portfolios; but this experiment was far from successful.
As administrators in the narrow sense, one proved to
be unusually good, several were fairly adequate, and
at least two were undoubted failures; but almost all
were deficient in general political capacity and sen-
sitiveness which no Minister, even under an omnipotent
War Cabinet, can lack with impunity.

But the device of a small executive body at the
head of affairs was an undoubted success, and it was
able to achieve results in every field of national
endeavour. It acted, rather than debated, and it gave
leadership and initiative at a time when the people
were feeling discouraged and fatigued with the strain
of war. "A change of government," said one of Mr.
Lloyd George's biographers, "acted like a new dress on
the spirits of a woman in the vapours, or like a brass
band on tired troops. The country simply wanted
rousing, and there was no man better fitted than Mr.
George to administer the necessary stimulus."[1] The
same writer describes how at the time of the crisis on
the Western front in 1918 the War Cabinet was able to
act promptly and effectively in securing the American
reinforcements and in providing without delay for their
transportation overseas:

We have here a good example of the very real virtues of
Mr. George's war control—virtues which compensated for
(as indeed they alone made possible) the persistence of much

[1] E. T. Raymond, *Mr. Lloyd George*, p. 225.

incidental inefficiency and extravagance. The abandonment of Cabinet responsibility, the latitude given to subordinates not always well chosen, was bound to result in much caprice. . . . But it had also the virtues of its defects. It might be wasteful, slovenly, inconsecutive . . . but it had also vision, vigour, high courage. . . . Once the Prime Minister had recognized that a thing must be done, he had only to give his orders, and it was done. This was the one superiority of the Cabal over the Sanhedrim. But it could be, on occasion, decisive.

Under Mr. Asquith's régime this question of the shipping for American troops would have been debated from every point of view. The shipping experts would have proclaimed it impossible; the naval experts would have stated all sorts of eloquent objections; the military experts would have condemned it as meaning no leave, the food experts as meaning no bread, the business experts as meaning no trade, the finance experts as meaning no revenue. After weeks of disputation on these lines Mr. Wilson would have been offered a quarter of the shipping they wanted, and meanwhile the Germans might well have got their decision. Mr. George arranged the affair in a few minutes, took all the responsibility on his own shoulders, and merely ordered his subordinates to do their part.[1]

The War Cabinet continued for about a year after the armistice; but it had ceased to operate as a separate body for some months before its final dissolution. Other Ministers attended its sessions in increasing numbers and participated in its deliberations, although they still took no formal responsibility for decisions. During this period several plans of reorganization were considered, ranging from two Cabinets, one for Imperial and one for Home Affairs, to the proposal seriously

[1] *Ibid*, pp. 254-6.

entertained by Lloyd George and Bonar Law to have no Cabinet at all during the Peace Conference. The King, we are told, was "greatly disturbed" by this radical suggestion, and it was eventually abandoned.[1] Finally, a return was made in the latter part of 1919 to the large Cabinet of earlier days, although a few of the war-time changes were retained. The secretariat had become invaluable; and its past achievements taken in conjunction with the great load of work carried by the post-war Cabinets made its abolition out of the question. It continued therefore to prepare the agenda and to record the conclusions of the Cabinet meetings, and also to notify formally the proper Ministers of all decisions which affected their departments.[2]

When the second great war broke out in 1939 one of the first acts of the Chamberlain Government was to reorganize the Cabinet. The official announcement was made that "the Prime Minister had decided to reconstitute the Government and set up a War Cabinet on the lines of the War Cabinet established in December, 1916."[3] The large ponderous body was once more discarded, and a new Cabinet of nine took its place. This was composed of the Prime Minister, the Chancellor of the Exchequer, the Foreign Secretary, the Lord Privy Seal, the heads of the three fighting services, the Co-ordinator of Defence, and

[1] Sir Austen Chamberlain, *Down the Years*, pp. 132-43.

[2] Only the Minister was henceforth notified, not the department; and only decisions of the Cabinet were recorded, not the discussion. W. I. Jennings, *Cabinet Government*, pp. 188-9, 212-13.

[3] *London Times*, Sept. 4, 1939.

Lord Hankey, the able Secretary of the previous War Cabinet, as a Minister without portfolio. Mr. Eden, as Secretary of State for the Dominions, was allowed to be in the Cabinet but not of it; he could attend its sittings in order to serve as a liaison officer with the Dominions, but he was not to be a regular member.

The most obvious comment is, of course, that this body is not at all a duplication of Mr. Lloyd George's War Cabinet.[1] It is, in the first place, twice the size of the earlier one; and hence it cannot be expected to be as speedy or as effective in the performance of certain of its executive functions. For the efficiency of a cabinet or any executive body, measured in terms of initiative and rapid decision, is intimately connected with its size: it might be said to vary in almost inverse geometric ratio to the number of members. "With a larger number of people," said Mr. Lloyd George years ago, "it meant so many men, so many minds; so many minds, so many tongues; so many tongues, so much confusion; so much confusion, so much delay."[2] While nine or ten councillors could scarcely be said to form a debating society, they are well beyond the maximum which will make quick and forceful action probable. One extraordinary duplication occurs in the presence of both the heads of the Admiralty, the Air Ministry, and the War Office, and the Minister for the Co-ordination of Defence, who is apparently in no way superior to those whose work he is supposed to co-ordinate. There would seem to be little reason why this gentle-

[1] The body of this essay was written before the fall of the Chamberlain Government.

[2] D. Lloyd George, *War Memoirs*, Vol. III, p. 1060.

man with the impressive title could not represent all the fighting services in the War Cabinet, and thus eliminate at one stroke three of the present members and reduce the total number to six or seven.[1] It is not without interest that only two months after the new Cabinet was constituted, the Prime Minister was compelled to deny in the House the existence within the War Cabinet of an inner executive, which was supposed to be directing the policies of the Government in secret.

But the present War Cabinet differs from its forbear in another and even more vital respect. Mr. Lloyd George planned a thinking organization, one which would not be mired in its own detailed administration and whose time and attention would be free to study the broad problems raised by the war. To this end he released four-fifths of its members from any departmental duties. Mr. Chamberlain and his assistants enjoy no such freedom. He himself continues to lead the House of Commons, and the heads of departments comprise six (or, with Mr. Eden, seven) more of the War Cabinet personnel. Yet all these are expected to add to their existing burdens the gigantic task of

---

[1] On April 3, 1940, the War Cabinet was reduced to eight members by the dropping of the Minister for the Co-ordination of Defence. At the same time the war effort of the government was placed in the hands of three key committees: the Service Ministers Committee, under Mr. Winston Churchill (the First Lord of the Admiralty); the Economic Policy Committee, under Sir John Simon (the Chancellor of the Exchequer); the Home Policy Committee, under Sir Kingsley Wood (the Lord Privy Seal). The change made Mr. Churchill the virtual Co-ordinator of Defence, left the Economic Committee as before (cf. *infra* pp. 192-4), and gave a little more unity to the other services. Some weeks later Mr. Churchill's powers were still further increased. Cf. Speech of Mr. Chamberlain, May 7, 1940.

directing the war activity of the whole British nation as well as that of a large part of the Empire.[1]

The War Cabinet, moreover, does not, like its predecessor, give any representation to the minority political parties.[2] Both the Labour and the Liberal Opposition were offered seats at its formation, the former apparently in the Cabinet, the latter in the Ministry; but each, believing that it would do more good by acting as a critic, declined to accept. Such an abstention undoubtedly detracts in some measure from the national character of the existing Government, although for the moment at least this does not appear to have had any serious consequences.

A much more formidable criticism is that the present organization does not make sufficient provision for coping with the multitude of economic and related problems which are indissolubly a part of modern warfare and with which no authority save a government is competent to deal. To what degree, for example, should the military policy of air raid precautions be allowed to interfere with the economic programme of intensified industrial activity? For defence purpose alone, the most extreme black-out regulations cannot be too drastic; but such regulations have already had disastrous effects on the production of munitions,

[1] Mr. Churchill's new Cabinet, formed on May 12, 1940, closely resembled that of Mr. Lloyd George in both the number of members and their freedom from departmental duties. The five members of this War Cabinet were: Prime Minister and Minister of Defence, Mr. Churchill; Lord President of the Council, Mr. Chamberlain; Lord Privy Seal, Mr. Atlee; Foreign Secretary, Viscount Halifax; Minister without portfolio, Mr. Greenwood.

[2] Mr. Churchill's War Cabinet contained two Labour members: the Ministry is composed of 39 Conservatives, 12 Labour, 7 Liberals, and 7 others whose party affiliations are doubtful.

aircraft, and many other essential commodities.[1] Some competent authority must obviously strike a balance between what must be in the nature of things conflicting policies. How, again, are the competing demands for both goods and labour to be reconciled? The army and navy and air force, the fighting services and the home front, production for domestic needs and for the export trade, the different industries throughout the country, all are pressing their rival claims for labour, food, clothing, and an infinite variety of goods which have but one thing in common—their supply is limited. Six Ministries deal almost exclusively with the economic side of the war, and no less than ten other Ministries are vitally concerned with economic matters. Again some authority must act as a mediator between both departments and industries and decide upon the priority which shall be given to each of these many competing demands as they arise. Moreover, such problems are never really settled; they fall, but to rise again, perhaps in the same form, perhaps in a different industry or with different commodities.

A further problem is that of timing, which involves difficulties closely allied to those of priorities. "At the Ministry of Munitions in the last war," writes Sir William Beveridge, "one of the most critical tasks was that of keeping different parts of production in step, as shortages occurred in turn. There was always some bottle-neck, but a different bottle-neck on each occasion. Dealing with bottle-necks in the organization of the whole economic effort of the nation at war,

[1] Cf. Sir William Beveridge, "War without Waste", (*London Times,* Oct. 3, 1939).

and securing the most effective distribution of resources in continually changing circumstances, is even more important and can be undertaken only by a central authority completely informed."[1]

These problems are, of course, being daily considered and decided by the existing government. A great number of questions are quickly settled by conferences between officials of different departments and through specialized committees at various points of contact. The more stubborn or more important questions go before two committees, one composed of civil servants, presided over by Lord Stamp, the other of Ministers under the Chairmanship of the Chancellor of the Exchequer:

The structure of the body which was to co-ordinate economic policy [explained the Chancellor of the Exchequer] might be described as a two-storey arrangement. On the ground floor was the inter-departmental committee over which Lord Stamp constantly presided. It included the permanent heads of Departments to which the economic problem of the war was of vital concern. It met constantly, and was concerned both with the regulation of current economic planning and with problems of a wider range which were the subject of planning for the future. The second storey consisted of Ministers, the political heads of the Departments, constituting a ministerial committee which was attended by Lord Stamp, who provided the essential connection between the two committees. He could assure the House that the machinery provided for the expeditious discussion of questions and for rapid decisions on important matters. . . .

In time of war they did not want to devote themselves too exclusively to the more theoretical or constitutional side of the

[1] *Ibid.*

matter. The real thing was to get a machine which did its work reasonably well. . . . The essential feature of this arrangement was that it preserved departmental and ministerial responsibility for certain aspects of Government policy. At the same time it brought together the co-ordination of demands and policy which otherwise might conflict, and brought to bear on that constant expert assistance.[1]

To many critics this arrangement appears to treat economic problems too casually. Their comprehensiveness and their vital importance is everywhere admitted, yet they are entrusted to an overburdened Chancellor of the Exchequer and to civil servants whose primary concern is in another and very much more restricted field. The only persons who are exclusively concerned with the broad questions of economic policy are Lord Stamp and the two economists who act as his assistants. Everyone else is engaged in specialized activity which is likely to narrow his outlook and engage his attention to such a degree that he will have little time to devote to the broad economic issues which are at least equally vital.[2] Moreover, the position of Lord Stamp, the cornerstone of the edifice, gives him little opportunity to co-ordinate the departmental work effectively.

He presides over the committee of officials, [writes Sir Arthur Salter] but does so without the reinforcement of continuous work between the meetings; he has access to the Cabinet Committee, but not on terms of equality as a Minister. Will the Departments be induced to subordinate their departmental policies by one who has the authority neither of a

[1] *London Times,* Oct. 19, 1939.

[2] Sir Arthur Salter, "Economic Strategy of the War" (*Contemporary Review,* Dec., 1939, pp. 641-8).

Minister nor of an executive official? It is difficult to believe that in the vast system this small element of unpreoccupied, disinterested, unbiased, co-ordinating authority is sufficient to develop and secure the enforcement of a real economic strategy. Nor can we expect the supreme function to be adequately discharged by a Chancellor of the Exchequer at the apex of the system, for he is preoccupied with his departmental duties; and the Treasury, though it has a more general survey than other Departments, still has its own departmental bias and outlook which may need to be not only co-ordinated with the needs of other offices but sometimes subordinated to them in the interests of a wider policy.[1]

Sir Arthur Salter's suggestion is to reduce the number of the War Cabinet and at the same time release its members from their load of departmental work, in other words, to return to a Cabinet resembling that of 1916-19. In this body, however, there would be a Minister explicitly responsible for economic affairs. The Minister would be advised by an economic general staff, composed of men like Lord Stamp, who would be without specialized duties and would devote their entire time to the work of co-ordination and planning for the future. The staff would keep in close touch with the activity and personnel of the different departments concerned with economic affairs, and would establish the same contact with them as the Treasury today has created with the financial officers of the spending departments. The Minister of Economic Co-ordination, like the present Chancellor of the Exchequer, would be expected to preside over the meetings of the Ministers whose departments were

[1] *Ibid*, p. 649.

involved in the economic problems of any given moment; while the head of the economic general staff would be, like Lord Stamp, chairman of his own group of officials.[1]

This scheme gives a fair idea of the kind of proposals which have been put forward by different people, and especially by the Labour party, during the past few months.[2] Most of the suggestions have had a common double purpose: the creation of a smaller and more effective Cabinet after the Lloyd George model, and the concentration to a much greater degree than heretofore on economic questions through the agency of skilled assistants and a special Ministry.[3] There is, of course, no reason to expect that the remedies of the last war have retained all their potency during the intervening twenty-five years and that they can be automatically prescribed to cope with present conditions; but there is equally no reason to believe that the earlier war experience is of no value in the existing emergency. The above suggestion, and others resembling it, seem to show a proper regard for the realities of the situation: they have endeavoured to utilize the valuable parts of the 1916 reforms, yet they have brought them more in line with modern needs. One bitter lesson at least might well be carried over

[1] *Ibid*, pp. 649-51.

[2] Sir William Beveridge, "War without Waste" (*London Times*, Oct. 3, 1939). H. J. Laski, "The Structure of the War Cabinet" (*New Statesmen and Nation*, Nov. 11, 1939). *King-Hall News Letter*, Dec. 8, 1939. "Real Economic Warfare", *London Times*, Nov. 30, 1939. *Labor Party Proposal* (E. Shinwell), *ibid.*, Oct. 19, 1939.

[3] Mr. Churchill's Cabinet followed the first of these suggestions, and will doubtless follow the second also.

from the last war, the folly of waiting until disasters and desperate circumstances compel the hasty adoption of changes which should have been made and could have been made years before.

The Canadian scene in both the last and the present war has naturally been much less disturbed than in Great Britain. The smallness of the country, the greater simplicity of its administrative machinery, its economic self-sufficiency, its relatively limited outside commitments, its infinitely narrower responsibilities, its geographical remoteness from the conflict—all have materially lessened the pressure on the Canadian government. Conditions have undoubtedly been difficult, and the executive, administrative, and legislative burdens have been enormously increased by the exigencies of war; but there has never been the same urgent necessity for fateful decision or immediate action which has rarely been absent from London. One result of this difference in conditions has been that Canada has been able to carry on her abnormal war activities with comparatively few structural changes in her government.

The Canadian Cabinet came through the last war almost intact. The addition of certain war activities and the formation of the Union Government substantially enlarged its numbers and led to the creation of a number of semi-independent boards which performed what would normally have been cabinet functions. One new Ministry, quite without precedent, was that of Overseas Military Forces, which was stationed in London and was charged with the welfare of the Canadian troops abroad, so far as that came under civil control. Another change was the appointment of three parliamentary under-secretaries, who were not in the Cabinet, but who had seats in the House and were able to relieve their respective Ministers of much work of secondary importance.

The most unusual departure took place at the time of the formation of the Union Government. The Cabinet was virtually divided into two large committees, each of nine members in addition to the Prime Minister who was the common Chairman. One of these committees, known as the War Committee, was composed of those Ministers primarily concerned with the prosecution of the war, and was designed to bring about closer co-ordination between their departments "to ensure the maximum of effort with a minimum of expenditure and generally to throw the full power of Canada into the war."[1] The second, called the Reconstruction and Development Committee, included the great majority of the remaining Ministers, such as those of Trade and Commerce, Agriculture, Interior, Immigration and Colonization, and Railways and Canals. The Order in Council creating this committee gave it a wide scope: the development of natural resources, general economic readjustments due to the war and the peace, transportation, labour problems, immigration—all these topics and more were entrusted to its care, chiefly for purposes of investigation and report.

These two committees had apparently no administrative powers of their own; they met to discuss problems, to act as a clearing house for suggestions and plans, and to apportion work among various other

[1] Sir Robert Borden, *Canadian House of Commons Debates,* March 19, 1918, p. 24.

bodies. They might themselves conduct enquiries or make decisions and submit their recommendations to Council; they might refer a matter to the appropriate department or departments for suitable action; they might appoint sub-committees of officials or laymen on any subject which required special investigation. The use of committees of the Cabinet is, of course, an old device, but this experiment had several novel features. The two bodies which have been described comprised almost the entire Cabinet; their creation was a deliberate effort to clear the Cabinet meetings of much of the routine and detailed problems which made such enormous inroads on the time and attention of its members; the topics assigned to the committees covered the whole sweep of administrative activity; the two bodies were focusing and supervising a far wider and more complex set of questions than any Canadian government had ever before attempted. There is some reason to believe that the results did not come entirely up to expectations; but the device certainly gave concentration and unity of effort at a time when these were very badly needed.

The coming of peace saw the Canadian Cabinet return gradually but completely to its pre-war structure and practice. The two large committees disappeared with the Armistice. The cessation of war activity, the retirement of weary Ministers, the dissolution of Union Government, and the accession of Mr. Meighen to the Prime Ministership reduced the size of the Cabinet from its maximum of twenty-one in 1918 to sixteen in 1920. The parliamentary under-secretaries were dropped by Mr. Meighen when he formed his first administration, were temporarily revived in one instance by Mr. Mackenzie King in the following year, and then, despite their many obvious advantages, permanently thrown into the discard. Three years after the Armistice scarcely a vestige of the war experience could be found in the national administration, save only a Pensions Board, a Department of Health, and a Minister of Finance whose task of balancing the budget had become much more onerous than ever before.

The present war, in Canada as in Great Britain, has been concerned to an unusual degree with economic problems, and this phase of the struggle has been the dominant influence in bringing about the many alterations which have been made in the structure of administration during the past few months. A large number of Cabinet committees have been constituted; boards and committees of civil servants have been created to deal with a wide variety of subjects; while a host of controllers, administrators, custodians, censors, registrars, and commissioners have been called into being to control, administer, ration, delete, protect, regulate, restrain, supervise, and generally to exercise authority over coal and wool, speeches and letters, stocks and bonds, pigs and people. Scarcely anyone in the Dominion knows what is going on or has been able to sort out or understand this bewildering jumble of positions and officials. The Government, animated by a commendable desire to inform the public, has issued a pamphlet entitled *War Organization: Cabinet Committees and Related Agencies,*[1] which enumerates at some length and with unusual obscurity many of these various offices and the supposed chain of authority

[1] King's Printer, Ottawa, 1940.

which joins them together. It is rumoured that the public demand for the pamphlet has not been large; but that the government departments themselves spend hours every day thumbing its pages and studying its impressive diagram in a vain endeavour to ascertain how this human jigsaw puzzle is fitted together.

The task of co-ordination and direction is, as usual, the vital one, and despite the many obscurities in this elaborate plan, the two bodies in the hierarchy which exercise the real power are discerned without much difficulty. The first is a small section of the Cabinet composed of the Prime Minister and five others,[1] who form a War Committee. This stands over ten other Cabinet committees which are placed in charge of such varied subjects as wheat, price control and labour, internal security, legislation, food production and marketing, etc. The second important body is known as the Advisory Committee on Economic Policy. It is made up of ten leading civil servants and bears a strong family resemblance to the committee of officials in Great Britain with Lord Stamp at its head. The Canadian Committee is supposed "to facilitate the work of the Committees of the Cabinet in the consideration of specific problems, to assist in avoiding duplication of effort by departments and agencies, and in furthering the effective co-ordination of economic and financial policy."[2] In short, members of the Advisory Committee keep in touch with all the war activities of the departments, boards and other agencies, smooth out difficulties, prepare questions for

[1] Government Leader in the Senate, and the Ministers of Finance, Justice, National Defence, and Mines and Resources.

[2] *War Organization: Cabinet Committees and Related Agencies*, p. 18.

the consideration of the Cabinet War Committee, and generally contrive to keep the machinery going with the minimum of friction.

It is probable that much of the paper organization is as yet disjointed and ineffective, although of this few can speak with certainty. For the perverted censorship which has excited the alarm and laughter of the nation has apparently beclouded many of these activities also, and Ottawa preserves an impressive silence on the subject of administrative dynamics. We are given a neat, concise pamphlet and a complicated chart, but virtually no inkling of the realities beneath this dull exterior. How can these dry bones be made to live? How seriously, for example, must one take the ten subsidiary Cabinet committees? Do they really have important functions? How often do they meet and how much do they decide? We can be reasonably sure, for example, that the Minister of National Defence cannot discharge all his enormous departmental functions and at the same time play a very active part on the vitally important central War Committee, the Committee on War Finance and Supply, the Committee on Shipping and Transportation, the Committee on Demobilization and Reestablishment, the Committee on Public Information, and the Committee on Internal Security, although the unfortunate Minister is a member of all these bodies. A possible answer is, of course, that these committees do very little and meet but rarely; and this surmise is to some degree confirmed by the fact that one of them, the Committee on Demobilization and Reestablishment by the very nature of its subject can scarcely be loaded with responsibilities at the present time. Such lapses from reality however, and the evident desire to make a good appearance not unnaturally raise the embarrassing question of the effectiveness of the entire organization.

Although it is admittedly difficult to criticize an institution where shadow and substance are so indistinguishably blended, the Canadian Cabinet presents other features which are clear and unmistakable and by no means above reproach. It is not easy, for example, to find any justification for the persistent disregard of such a well tried device as the use of parliamentary under-secretaries to relieve Ministers of excessive work and detail. They have been used in Great Britain for generations; they were recommended in Canada by Sir George Murray in 1912[1] and by a Senate Committee in 1919;[2] they have been repeatedly endorsed by the present Prime Minister;[3] they were tried with marked success in Canada in the nineties and during the last war. "My only regret", said Sir Robert Borden in 1917, "is that I did not take steps early in the war to have an Under-Secretary of State for External Affairs appointed; it would have been better for the interests of the country had I done so. I would have had more time to give to general considerations; my attention would not have been so much taken up with matters which, though important, were nevertheless of a some what routine character."[4]

[1] *Canadian Sessional Papers*, 1913, No. 57a.

[2] *Report of the Special Committee of the Senate on the Machinery of Government, Canadian Senate Journals*, 1919, p. 346.

[3] *Toronto Globe*, Dec. 30, 1921. *Saskatoon Star Phoenix*, Oct. 25, 1935.

[4] *Canadian House of Commons Debates*, Aug. 7, 1917, p. 4205.

The same reasoning applied to the Cabinet as a whole would indicate the desirability of instituting a body of the type of Mr. Lloyd George's War Cabinet of 1916 composed of a few members untrammelled by departmental duties. The present Canadian War Committee would thus be a convenient size but only one member, the Senate representative, is without portfolio. It is difficult to understand how the Committee's work of making rapid decisions, of planning for the future, and of co-ordinating the many activities of the departments and other agencies, can be conducted with reasonable care or efficiency when its members are saddled with a load of departmental responsibilities. Moreover, this Committee has not, in theory at least, supplanted the Cabinet; and it is quite conceivable that the two bodies may not find it easy to co-operate as freely as is desirable. If, however, the Committee has in effect become the Government, then it would be better to face the facts, and organize both Cabinet and Ministry in accordance with their new relationship.

Canada has also seen fit to disregard entirely the British experience regarding the organization of Cabinet business—an experience which is, after all, founded on the most elementary common sense. The lack of any secretarial staff, the neglect of carefully prepared agenda, the absence of any formal record of Cabinet decisions would of themselves be serious enough to make a change highly desirable; but the British example in the last war and during the succeeding period should have made a change irresistible. Yet after twenty-four years of successful experience in

Britain, we have not been prepared to risk what is, after all, the mildest and least venturesome of political experiments.[1]

The last war produced another Cabinet which has not hitherto been mentioned, namely, the Imperial War Cabinet. For over two years Canada was at war without having any voice whatever in the formulation or direction of Empire policy, during which time the protests of Sir Robert Borden were received with the utmost courtesy combined with expressions of profound regret that no solution of the difficulty could be found.[2] But only a week after Mr. Lloyd George had become Prime Minister and formed his small War Cabinet of five, he took the further step of summoning the Dominion Prime Ministers to London. The result of this summons was the formation of the Imperial War Cabinet, which held its first meeting in March 1917. It was composed of the British War Cabinet, the Dominion Prime Ministers or their representatives, a member from India, and the Colonial Secretary who spoke for the Crown Colonies. Imperial Conferences had frequently been held before the war, and another one was in fact also held on this occasion; but the Imperial War Cabinet was an entirely new experiment, unknown in Empire history. It differed from the Conference in both personnel and function; it was a much smaller body, and it exercised executive instead of merely consultative powers. "The Crown at present", said Sir Robert Borden, "acts upon the

[1] On April 9, 1940, a Minister of Supply was appointed to take charge of the purchases of war supplies. In recent months a secretariat is gradually being built up as the need for such a body becomes more and more apparent.

[2] *Robert Laird Borden, His Memoirs*, Vol. II, pp. 620-4.

advice of a Cabinet in all Imperial matters, which includes not only Ministers responsible to the British Parliament but also those responsible to the Parliaments and Governments of the respective Dominions."[1] The Imperial War Cabinet remained in session for two months; it met again in the summer of 1918 for a longer period; and later in that year, masquerading as the British Empire Delegation, it went to Paris and helped negotiate the peace treaty.

Its record during these years indicates in no uncertain manner its exceptional importance. It enabled the Dominions to participate in the determination of Empire policy, and it also gave them a protection and control over their own interests which at times was badly needed. Its members were given access to all British cabinet documents; they decided various questions concerned with foreign policy, the prosecution of the war, the terms of peace, and the means of co-operation with the Allies; they were constantly receiving confidential reports from the Admiralty, the General Staff, and the Commander-in-Chief; and they took part in all conferences with military and naval officers.[2] Borden was compelled on several occasions to intervene in what he considered to be infractions of Canada rights, such as an interference with Canadian forestry battalions and an effort to merge the Canadian Corps with the British Army. When in 1918 he became convinced of the inefficiency of the British generals he did not hesitate to send for Sir Arthur Currie and demand from him the truth

[1] Report of Imperial War Conference, 1917, *Parl. Pap.* (*Great Britain*) 1917, Cd. 8566, p. 59.

[2] *Robert Laird Borden, His Memoirs,* Vol. II, pp. 678-9, 683, 836.

about the actual conditions in France and insist on a frank statement of the causes of failure. Armed with this information, he denounced in the War Cabinet "the incompetency, disorganization and confusion at the Front," and secured as a result a special committee of Prime Ministers to survey the whole field of war activity. The report of this committee, however, was rendered unnecessary and obsolete by the coming of the Armistice.[1]

In 1921 an attempt was made to revive the Imperial Cabinet and use it as the source of joint Empire action on foreign affairs; but the centrifugal forces had by this time become too powerful, and the Dominions showed little desire to mix in the world-wide problems of Great Britain. The Imperial Cabinet idea was therefore dropped, although occasional meetings of the Imperial Conference continued to take place as before.

A month after the outbreak of the present war it was announced that the Dominions would each send a Cabinet Minister to London to confer with the British Government "on the best method of co-ordinating the resources of the Empire for War" although, said Mr. Anthony Eden, the Secretary of State for the Dominions, there would be "no question of departing from the well-established constitutional principle of the British Commonwealth that executive responsibility will remain with the several Governments individually."[2] In short, an emergency consultation would be held, but it was not in any way to be construed as a modern version of the Imperial War Cabinet. The meeting took place in October and

[1] *Ibid.*, Vol. II, pp. 811-14.
[2] *London Times*, Oct. 5, 1939.

November of last year; Ministers arrived with their military and economic experts; many valuable conferences were held with the British authorities and with one another; they inspected the Maginot line; they were received by the French Prime Minister and were dined at the British Embassy in Paris. "Their trip to France," Mr. Eden announced, "alone would have justified their visit to Europe, and each Minister would be able to return to his Dominion with a message of strong encouragement."[1] In short, it was apparently a very profitable meeting for everyone; and the Ministers were able to absorb some information and a great deal of enthusiasm.

Any proposal to revive a genuinely consultative and executive body such as the Imperial War Cabinet has so far met with little support in either Great Britain or the Dominions. Mr. Eden's announcement of the gathering a few months ago denied the idea by implication; and Mr. Mackenzie King stated explicitly at the same time that this meeting was to be neither an Imperial Cabinet nor an Imperial Conference. The British seem to be assuming the comfortable position that now that the Dominions are completely self-governing, they will not want any Imperial Cabinet, but presumably will be more willing than ever before to do nothing except consult and co-operate. "We have not revived the Imperial War Cabinet of twenty years ago," runs a *Times* editorial, "it is already clear that informal consultations, such as are about to be opened will serve the purpose better."[2] *The Round Table* states that "Ministers

[1] *Ibid*, Nov. 14, 1939.
[2] Nov. 1, 1939, editorial.

from all the Dominions have already arrived in London, not to constitute as in the last war an 'Imperial War Cabinet'—that was always a misnomer and is not needed now—but for consultation with British Ministers which will be none the less close and effective because it is informal."[1]   And the *Times* once again:

> Still less is there any occasion at present, even if it were practicable, to include the statesmen of the Dominions in a central War Cabinet in London.   It is not that such men as Mr. Menzies or General Smuts, for example, would not be a tower of strength, as individuals, in any council.   But the Dominions have grown apace since their leaders last sat in Downing Street.   Their position is not more detached from British interests, but it is different; and their Prime Ministers at all events have urgent responsibilities in their own countries in preparing for a war in which no man can predict the range.   It is good news that they may be able to visit this country after the turn of the year, but for the rest they can undoubtedly do better work for the Empire where they are.[2]

Is this situation, after all, very different from that complained of so bitterly by Sir Robert Borden in 1915 and 1916?   In the last war the Dominions were so unimportant that their advice was not considered necessary; in this war, their contribution is of such vital consequence that they cannot well afford to scatter their energies by attending meetings of the Imperial Cabinet.   The net result is apparently the same.   Mr. Bonar Law on the earlier occasion said that he was only too delighted to give Sir Robert

[1] December 1939, p. 14.
[2] Oct. 6, 1939, editorial.

Borden all the information possible and at one time he even sent him a special mail bag, weighted with lead and bulging with confidential documents.[1] But when effective consultation was suggested, the British Government found itself unable for over two years to devise any system to meet the problem. Today Mr. Anthony Eden has become another fountain of information; and although he is doubtless a little more generous with his material than Mr. Bonar Law, Canada is apparently expected to be willing once more to acquiesce in policies already made and plans already undertaken. Curiously enough, there has been as yet no substantial complaint about the absurdity of the situation. It is true that the Dominions have for twenty years steadily avoided close co-operation, and stressed autonomy and independence; but under the present abnormal circumstances they could demand, without any inconsistency, a temporary return to some consultative arrangement such as the old Imperial War Cabinet. Hitherto the policies of Great Britain and the Dominions might, and frequently did, diverge and differ, but today they must necessarily be identical in virtually every respect. The declaration of war by the Dominions has led to their particular foreign interests being almost completely blended with those of the other parts of the Empire; and none of them can afford to sit back and allow the British Government to determine Empire

[1] Mr. Bonar Law wrote Sir Robert that they were very confidential indeed and must be read by himself alone; then he underlined this caution; and later, thinking the Prime Minister a bit dull, he repeated the same words in a foot-note. Borden got his revenge rather neatly by cabling for permission to show them to the Governor-General; but it is to be feared that Bonar Law missed the point. *Robert Laird Borden: His Memoirs*, Vol. II, pp. 623-4.

policies which are bound to affect them all so intimately.

Mr. Crerar's little trip and consultation of last
autumn bore slight resemblance to the manifold
activities of the Imperial War Cabinet twenty years
ago. The recent consultation was probably very
useful, and it did, no doubt, do much to bring about
closer understanding of the common problems of
Great Britain and the Dominions and ensure more
intelligent co-operation amongst their governments.
But such an informal delegation could never come to
grips with the the really vital war problems in which
the interests of the Dominions are immediately
concerned. What remedy will be available if there
is another attempt to interfere with Canadian troops?
Is Great Britain alone to have the authority to settle
the vexed questions which are apt to arise between the
civil and military power? Will there be a pool of the
material resources of the Empire, but no pool of its
political talent or its executive capacity? It is difficult
to suppose that Canada is prepared to repeat the
sacrifices of twenty-five years ago, yet would be willing
to exercise no control over the strategy of war or
the conditions of peace. For months the British
Government decided on its own responsibility or, in
many instances, with French co-operation, such
questions as the attitude of the Empire towards Russia,
the aiding of Finland, the treatment of German
exports, the censorship of American mails and the oil
issue in Roumania. Every one of these problems
has a direct bearing on the war and is a matter of
great consequence to every Dominion; some of them
may quite conceivably result in prolonging or short-

ening the struggle or even determining a Dominion's future political existence. Yet on all these questions no Dominion has been taken into consultation, no Dominion has played more than the purely passive role of receiving such information as the British Cabinet chooses to disclose. "Is this war being waged by the United Kingdom alone," asked Sir Robert Borden, "or is it a war waged by the Empire?" This question, now as in 1916, cannot long remain unanswered.

VIII. DEMOCRACY IN THE OVERSEAS DOMINIONS

by ALEXANDER BRADY

IN certain obvious respects the Dominions are alike. They all contain large and sparsely settled territories, where politics and social life have been penetrated in various degrees with the spirit of the frontier. They possess a peculiar intimacy of relations with two older and highly developed communities, Great Britain and (to a less degree) the United States—an intimacy which facilitates cultural borrowing. They inherited from colonial times the same traditions and techniques of parliamentary rule. And in all of them the evolution of parliamentarianism has taken a somewhat like course: the common intense devotion to party leaders, the growing tendency to exalt the cabinet at the expense of the representative body, the increasing confidence in the departmental mind, the capacity of political parties to adopt and to perpetuate the measures of opponents, and generally to trust the test of experience. Moreover, throughout the dominions the structure of social classes is relatively flexible; more so than in Great Britain, for the Englishman's class system, with all its sturdiness, was not readily exportable. Conditions of life on cattle ranches, sheep stations or the mushroom towns of a new country soon destroyed the social distinctions of the immigrant, and opened the way to that egalitarian liberalism, with its roots in three centuries of British history, which grew most readily in Britain's nineteenth century colonies.

These similarities in the dominions enable public men to speak a common political language, however different in accent and import, understood in Ottawa, Canberra and Pretoria. And they must be reckoned as significant among the bonds of association which make possible the present British Commonwealth and which may perhaps largely determine its fate.

But the distinctions between the dominions are as notable as their similarities. These pertain less to the mechanisms of the parliamentary system than to the extra-legal portion of government, the nature and functioning of parties, the racial and cultural structure of the country, the social and economic problems with which government has to cope, and hence the immediate goal whither the dominion is directed by the pressure of its environment. With some of these distinctions this essay is concerned, beginning with the salient features of Canadian democracy.

While Canada was a pioneer in colonial self-government, yet after achieving autonomy, it was slower and more cautious than the antipodean colonies in its experiments in political democracy; especially slower in moving towards social democracy. To Australia and New Zealand, not to Canada, itinerant sociologists from Europe went in the nineties to examine the most recent ventures in social legislation. The issues of Canadian politics did not then turn on such problems as compulsory industrial arbitration, minimum wages, and old age pensions, but rather on the rights of race or church, the expediency of tariff changes (the contentious issue between the interests of farm and factory), and the ever absorbing question of railway transport. "Consult the annals of Canada for the past fifty years at random", wrote Paul Lamarche in 1917, "and whatever party may be in power, what do you find? The government is building a railway, buying a railway, selling a railway, or blocking a railway."

Not indeed until after the last war did Canadian governments become deeply concerned with the initial aims and mechanisms of modern social legislation; e.g., nearly thirty years after the Fabian, William Pember Reeves, had begun to draft and to establish an advanced code of social services for New Zealand, and an equal period after the Labour Party had entered politics in Australia with the aim of social amelioration. The more obvious reasons for this tardiness are found in the peculiar facts of Canadian industrial structure which weakened the pressures for social experimentation. Chief among these has been the agrarian basis of the community.

In Canada parliamentary rule originated in a society which resembled the United States when popular institutions took form in what Turner and his school called "the frontier." While modified by special circumstances, particularly by the presence in the population of the contrasting cultures of French and British, Canadian institutions were conditioned by social forces similar to those in the neighbouring republic. Here prominently was even the individualist Puritan spirit, so significant in the northern United States. Canadian democracy at the outset and for long rested on a class of yeomen. Its vitality was drawn from small farmers, independent or striving to be independent, and seeing in franchises, legislatures and responsible executives the political order calculated to further their interests. Their concern as a class was free access to the land, ready markets, means of getting to markets, monetary and financial policies advantageous to their economy, and protection against urban interests that might menace them. They had no concern with social services in the modern sense of the term; e.g., services which inevitably have the effect of redistributing wealth. The family-farm, as the basic economic and social unit, provided within its own fences security to its aged, injured or unemployed. The idea of a state redirecting the flow of income to relieve the accidents of fortune clashed with the deepest prejudices of agrarian democrats. The Jeffersonian concept of a "diminished state" was clearly interwoven in the thought of the Canadian yeomen who fought the cause of responsible government. A convention of the Grits in the fifties formulated the resolution: "Give the government as little to do as possible, and that clearly defined."

This view underwent some but no drastic revision between the middle of the 19th century and the war of 1914. Subsidizing and building of railways by government were, as a departure from the principle, readily made acceptable to the farmers—the dominant portion of the electorate—as a means of opening access to additional land or of improving the prospects of markets. Thus, the rural interests appeared to coincide with the commercial and industrial interests of the towns. Even a purely agrarian party, such as the

Patrons of Industry in the nineties, which like the Populists of the United States sought to forge bonds of union between farmers and organized labour, would assign to government no elaborate economic and social functions. They demanded some control over public utilities to prevent the private companies from exploiting the farmer and the general public, a low tariff, legislation against combines, more direct democracy (abolition of the senate and direct election of county officials, etc.), and greater economy and purity in administration. In this, the advanced reform programme of the period, no requests significantly were made for what could properly be called social services. Yet in the same decade important parties emphasizing social reform arose in other parts of the Empire.

The Patrons were simply faithful to the traditional ideals of agrarian democracy. Fidelity to these ideals, whether in the national parties or in special associations, continued to characterize the agrarian interest to the last war and even beyond. It is a commonplace that the war was a turning-point in the country's development; not least a turning-point in the forces that fashion Canadian democracy. It quickened previous tendencies to urban industrialism, with a resulting shift of political power from the country to the town. In 1901, 62 persons in every 100 of the total population lived in rural areas; in 1921, 50 in every 100. The percentage of population gainfully employed in agriculture similarly shrank. But the arrangement of the constituencies continued to be such as always to give a greater weight to the rural vote. As the agrarian influence declined, the new urban pressures—aided sometimes as in the West by agrarians who were changing their philosophy of the State—expressed itself in the post-war period in a growing code of social services; most of them administered by the provinces. This development would doubtless have been more rapid but for the lack of cohesion in urban forces. Organized labour, for example, has been singularly weak, split between French-speaking and English-speaking groups, with divergent doctrines of action; between national and international organizations; and hampered also by regionalism and the geographic difficulties which confront all dominion movements. Roughly indicative of labour's relative weakness is the fact that by 1937 about *one* Canadian in every *twenty-eight* was a trade unionist as compared with *one* in every *seven* in Australia, and *one* in every *eight* in New Zealand. Moreover the organized workers of the town obtain no reinforcement from the country. The family-farm as the central fact in the agrarian economy means the absence of a rural proletariat of any significance. Mechanization has reduced even what casual labour used to be employed at certain seasons. Labour, beyond what is carried out by members of the family, is performed by "the hired man", and in him there is none of the potentialities of a trade unionist.

Political parties are the most reliable reflectors of democratic forces, and significantly since the last war they have retained that substantially composite character developed in the formative period of the country's history, seeking to represent the main races, religions and regions; breaking socially on vertical rather than horizontal lines. While they reflect the new urban impulses, the economic fact of the family farm and its cultural life—a life especially in Quebec rooted deep in tradition—still profoundly influences their behaviour and policies, whether in negation or in positive action. The one fresh incident of significance was the emergence of the C. C. F. (Canadian Commonwealth Federation), which in seeking to be a successful combination of farmers and labour was not entirely new—the Patrons pursued that aim forty years ago. But it has failed in its attempt, for it has been little more than a number of regional parties under one label; agrarian on the prairie, mainly urban in British Columbia and Ontario, and with little appeal at all east of the Ottawa. Agrarians naturally approved of some of the economic policies which the party promised, especially those on banking and credit; they were also interested in government assistance to co-operatives. Labour's chief interest was in social services, although some of the leaders combined with Fabian-minded intellectuals often spoke in terms of nationalizing industry and achieving socialism. Such talk thoroughly frightened the farmers in eastern Canada, and, in less than a year after the framing of the Regina Programme, the United Farmers of Ontario withdrew their affiiliation with the C. C. F. In the west the farmers were less disturbed by urban radicalism. Yet even there the effort to unite rural and urban forces in a semi-socialist movement strained agrarian loyalty and not a little explained Mr. Aberhart's triumph in 1935. A Social Credit Messiah made more appeal to the farmer's mind than Socialism.

Nothing short of changes disruptive of the whole family-farm economy were likely in that period, or in any other, to evoke a ready response to new political and social aims. That fact lends unity to agrarianism from early colonial times, and combined with the weakness of trade unionism and the deeply entrenched power of urban financiers and manufacturers explain why the impulses towards social democracy in Canada have been relatively weak.

Australia's democratic development has differed from that of Canada. The country was never a yeoman democracy, for the controls of geography determined that Australia could not become a small farmer state. From the day that John Macarthur undertook to prove that Australia's wealth lay in sheep, not in crops, the course of the country's social development was determined. By 1850 Australian merinos were producing more than one-half of the total British imports of wool, a fact which translated into social results meant the rise of the pastoralist with his flocks and employed workers, herdsmen, boundary-riders and once a year the skilled craftsmen of pastoralism, the shearers. Zealous efforts of the British colonial authorities to achieve a concentrated settlement were broken by the hostile forces of physical environment. In a country of light rainfall and rapid evaporation, extensive rather than intensive grazing lands were essential; the main expansion of wool-growing could take place only through the occupation of fresh acres. Hence the pastoralists with their flocks set out into the interior, crossing mountains and sun-baked plains always in search of fertile valleys that would provide fresh grazing. Such were the squatters of Australian history; a class dominant in the first half of the nineteenth century, and distingushed from the small farmers whose humble pioneering tasks constitute the chronicle of Canadian settlement and out of whose political efforts emerged our democracy.

The self-government which came in the forties and fifties was at the outset squattercratic rather than democratic. The squatters fought its cause, and seemed destined to reap its benefits but for the alluvial gold-rushes of the fifties, which brought three-quarters of a million immigrants and destroyed "the realization of the squatter's dream."[1] The digger tradition, product of the gold-rush era, was liberal in the egalitarian sense, and stood for an aggressive expression of the popular will in government. In brief, shortly after the mid-period of the century, the characteristic impulses of Australian democracy were already evident. In determining those impulses, the social elements in the flow of immigration had significance. There were a goodly number of Irish nationalists of the 1848 vintage, who did not refrain under Australian skies from indulging in intense political struggle, which in the national tradition has been a reasonably good substitute for tribal warfare. Their influence was thrown emphatically in the scale against the domination of large land owners.

Chartists also entered the country, and the realization of the six points became an Australian ideal that was much sooner realized than in England or in Canada. Vote by ballot, for example, was established in Victoria in 1858; fourteen years before its enactment by Gladstone, sixteen years before Canada adopted it.

[1] The point is excellently but briefly illustrated by Professor G. V. Portus, *Australia: An Economic Interpretation* (Sydney, 1933).

The principle of paying members of the legislature was accepted by Victoria in 1878; British democracy fought for it throughout another generation. South Australia gave women the parliamentary vote in 1895; the women in England and Canada were denied it till the war of 1914. And so on, the chronicle of expanding political franchises might be extended. As Australians early won political privileges, evidently also they early lost interest in them, for Queensland in 1915 tried out compulsory voting, followed by the Commonwealth in 1924. In Canada compulsory voting has remained up to the present only a matter of desultory discussion.

The first impulses towards social democracy followed closely upon the achievement of political liberties, and here the contrast with Canada is even more marked. The circumstances which encouraged these impulses were related to the gold industry, pastoralism, and urban growth. Alluvial gold was soon succeeded by quartz mining which did not attract the man of small means. Thousands of migrants to the gold diggings were now cut adrift, dependent upon employment offered by other industries. In a pastoral country divided into great holdings, scattered thinly with cattle and sheep, the workers were forced to move from job to job, with scant hope of attaining independence. The sharp contrast between the search for Eldorado and the hard struggle for employment fostered ideas, especially a passion for social equality, which have characterized Australian democracy ever since. A product of the era, Joseph Furphy, in his novel *Such is Life*, has depicted for history the spirit of "mateship" of struggling, unsettled station hands, sundowners, knockabout bushmen, sons of unlucky gold-seekers and hopeful immigrants.[1] This restless humanity was the equivalent of America's frontier democracy, but, thanks to the physical character of the country, it was not in the same degree swarming into homesteads; it was more genuinely proletarian, and hence it tended soon to assist those political thrusts in the direction of social democracy, evident by the turn of the century.

The continued utilization of the land for grazing favoured the same development, for it tended both to diffuse and to concentrate population. It has, in contrast to the utilizing of agrarian lands in most parts of Canada, scattered population in the settled part of the interior, restricted the number and growth of small towns, and by contrast centralized a considerable proportion of the trading and industrial population at the large metropolitan ports, such as Sydney and Melbourne. Owing to these facts Australia early in the last century began to develop that trait of advanced metropolitanism revealed so notably today. In four of the six states approximately 50 per cent. of the people are to be found in the metropolitan centres, and in the country as a whole the urban population is about 64 per cent. of the total, compared with some 53 per cent. in Canada. Urbanization has facilitated trade unionism, and in the absence of disintegrating factors, such as cleavages of race and language, trade unionism grew with firmer cohesion than in this country.

Moreover pastoralism means advanced capitalism on the land, involving inevitably a rural proletariat, and giving rise to a phenomenon little known in

---

[1] Vance Palmer (ed.), *Such is Life*, Being Certain Extracts from the Diary of Tom Collins (London, 1937).

Canada, rural trade unionism. The unions of the country linked with those of the town presented a singularly united front of organized workers, and made possible effective participation of labour in politics when once the framework of political democracy was complete. Within the first decade of the present century, labour parties had achieved power in the Commonwealth and in some of the leading states, and their pressure irresistibly directed legislation towards social services, extensive controls over industry, and state ownership and operation of major public utilities. Admittedly much of the public ownership and operation, often described in the Antipodes as "State Socialism", is not attributable simply or even considerably to the democratic pressures or social theory of organized labour, but, as in other dominions, to the exigencies of colonization; to the practical consideration that a pioneer community in a remote portion of the globe can best attract capital when government is the borrower. The influence of the labour parties in Australia, with a socialist tinge to their thought, has been directed to enlarging the range of government activity beyond the necessities of colonization. Hence the experiments in the public management not merely of railways and steamships, but of hotels, banks, life insurance, sawmills, brickworks, and for a time (in Queensland) cattle stations and meat shops. Through this widening circle of control, the Commonwealth and its states have become one of the most advanced laboratories of public administration under parliamentary democracy in the world.

But the most distinctive feature of Australian social experiment, with which Canada has no close parallel, is the system of industrial control operative in wage-fixing and compulsory arbitration. Here the states as well as the Commonwealth have developed an elaborate structure of law and institution whose primary function is to secure the Australian standard of living. Hence it is supplemented by protection and rigid immigration restriction. Indeed it is but one stone in an elaborate arch of economic control. Important as are the tribunals which prescribe the basic wage for industries within the states, the Commonwealth Arbitration Court assumes pride of place, not merely because at least 20 per cent. of the Australian labour force directly accept its awards (the percentage increases), but because its deliberations and decisions influence other wage-fixing bodies. Established as experimental in 1904, it has matured, as one of the most interesting industrial courts in the world, to its present firmly entrenched position in the socio-economic structure of the Australian Commonwealth. This venture of jurisprudence to reduce industrial warfare and to maintain acceptable standards of living by judicial award has not escaped criticism. Rather it has worked in an atmosphere of continuous debate for and against. Yet the majority of Australian working-men seem to be convinced that judicial arbitration is the sheet anchor of their social security, and a government promptly lost power in 1929 when it threatened the Commonwealth system.

On parliamentary politics in Australia—the functioning of parties, legislatures and civil services—many points of significant comparison and contrast with Canada are evident. One alone need be emphasized; viz., the prominent rôle of a disciplined labour party, resting on trade unionism. This is the source of most that is distinctive in Australian politics. The social goals of the democracy are in a goodly part those of trade unionists. The techniques of political action are likewise fashioned, and there is introduced to political warfare a sharper and more undisguised sense of class interest than is customary in Canada. The effort of the trade unionist to control the labour politician has led to the intricate structure of the party, with its pledges, platforms, state conferences, and caucuses. The effort to hold leaders strictly responsible to the rank and file has made Australian labour politics the history of periodic internal conflicts and secessions. Of *eleven* Prime Ministers since the birth of the Commonwealth, *three* have been ex-members of the Labour Party, who had either seceded or been expelled.

Despite recurring tensions the party remains an effective instrument, not merely in maintaining and furthering Australia's type of democracy; but also in lending to the politics of a large country a peculiar unity, for it seeks in all the states a social objective that cuts across, perhaps more clearly than that of any other party, the narrower aims of geographic sections. In the last forty-odd years it has derived a dynamic cohesion from its social ideal, and has imparted something of that cohesion to the entire Commonwealth. Yet its own unity would be impossible but for the racial and cultural homogeneity of the community, contrasting with the diversity in Canada and South Africa. Australians have a sound instinct in emphasizing the importance of their "ninety-odd" per cent. British.

In many social and political respects New Zealand resembles Australia. Its population also is dominantly British in extraction, and hence it has been little

troubled by the issues of minority races which impair
the social cohesion of Canada and South Africa. (The
Maoris represent only 5 per cent. of the population.)
Like most Australian states, its development began
when liberalism was asserting a hold upon the mind
and colonial policies of Great Britain. It received in
infancy the solicitous attentions of many, not least
Gibbon Wakefield, who sought to make it a new
England in the Pacific, but unlike the old England nur-
tured fully from birth on a Benthamite diet. Here as
in Australia, alluvial gold in the sixties helped to attract
immigrants in whom the democratic impulse was
powerful. Not surprisingly, therefore, it early implemented the principal demands of the Chartists, and
went beyond "the six points" by being the first part of
the British empire to face the perils of enfranchising
women. Also like the Australian states, it was not long
content with the forms of political democracy, but
proceeded in the nineties of the last century to
elaborate an advanced code of social and industrial
legislation. In some matters, New Zealand gave the
lead to Australia. It was the pioneer in establishing
compulsory industrial arbitration and old-age pensions.
The famous British Education Act of 1902 was partly
influenced by a Fabian tract, *The Education Muddle
and the Way Out,* written by William Pember Reeves,
a former minister of the Crown in New Zealand, where
he had discovered "the way out", which he urged with
success upon the British.[1] Nor is it small testimony to
the country's triumphant humanitarianism that by
energetic attention to public health, it achieved the

[1] W. K. Hancock, "England and Australia: A Study in Democratic
Development", *Nineteenth Century,* July, 1933.

lowest infantile death-rate in the world. In brief, for some fifty years of its century (reached in 1940), New Zealand like Australia has been headed in the direction of social democracy; perhaps never more so than under the present régime of the Labour Party.

Yet the similarities in democratic development between New Zealand and Australia must not obscure significant differences. The smallness of the islands as compared with the neighbouring continent destroyed any argument for federalism despite the strength of local feeling. Consequently the democracy has not been restrained and embarrassed by the rigidities of a federal constitution. The popular will has had more complete scope to express itself, and one may readily hazard the view that, without the unitary system, the dominion's record in social legislation would have been less impressive. Perhaps more important is its difference from most parts of Australia in that climatic and physiographic features favoured a class of small farmers. But, as a small farmer democracy, New Zealand has been distinguished by extending the principle of social amelioration and wide government activity in the economic field as far at least as any similar country in the world.

The phenomenon of a powerful agrarian electorate maintaining extensive social services is the product of peculiar historical circumstances. In the nineteenth century even the fostering care of Benthamite god-parents did not save New Zealand from a policy that resulted in the alienation of vast tracts of its best land to wool-kings and corporations. The story is too involved to be told here, beyond pointing out that by the eighties land monopolization was viewed by the masses as an evil of the first magnitude. An unusually intense depression accentuated the discontent of the landless and wageless, and led to the triumph of a Liberal party in 1891, with a programme designed to place the small man on the land and to bring security to the labourer. Aggressive democracy was born in New Zealand mainly in this struggle for the land. Breaking the power of the large landowners was impossible without the voting power of the labourers, a power which was won only by the promise and achievement of social services. Thus, there was achieved one of the few effective alliances in the history of the dominions between small farmers and labour.

The Liberal party held office from 1891 to 1912. Their period of most active reform was the nineties, when they were led by an ex-miner, Lancashire-born, Richard Seddon; a man of unbounded optimism who was aptly described as having had "an unrivalled capacity for identifying the workings of the Deity with the politics of New Zealand".[1] Legislation to establish in security a small farmer class involved much that was enterprising; e.g., graduated taxation of the unimproved value of land (Henry George had visited New Zealand in 1889), compulsory subdivision of large estates into farms of small holders, and limitation for the future of the amount of Crown land to be acquired by any individual. But perhaps more important than anything placed upon the statute books was the upward trend in prices of agricultural products combined with the success of refrigeration on ships which made it possible and profitable for the small farmer to produce for the British market. At any rate Liberalism was

[1] J. C. Beaglehole, *New Zealand: A Short History* (1936), 57.

successful. It achieved its end, and in doing so helped to destroy itself. As the class of small farmers grew in number and prosperity, it became less interested in the social policy of the Liberals. The latter consequently slackened the pace of social experimentation, lost the support of labour, and in 1912 fell from power.

Fortunately, although little was added to the structure of social and industrial legislation drafted with masterly care by William Pember Reeves, the product of the reforming zeal of the nineties survived. André Siegfried and other sociologists from Europe, visitors to the country in its heyday of reform, would have had little sociological reason to make a return visit till 1935, when the Labour Party for the first time came to power, with a plan and with impressive determination. The plan embraced four related and far-reaching ends: a more even distribution of wealth, an improvement in the working conditions of the employees, an increase in the national income, and a smoothing out of sharp fluctuations in the flow of income. The scheme of legislation which followed in the succeeding two years laid a particular emphasis upon a more equitable distribution of wealth and the re-establishment of a more adequate system of industrial control through the Arbitration Court. Thus, old age pensions, payable to women at 60 and men at 65, were increased; pensions for widows with dependent children were placed on a more generous basis; family allowances, cut in the depression, were restored; relief payments to unemployed were enlarged; wages and salaries of public servants were restored to their pre-depression level (they had been cut by the previous government); wage rates of workers under awards of the arbitration court were increased; and the power of the court was enlarged in order that it could "fix basic rates of wages at a level sufficient to enable adult male workers to maintain a wife and three children in a fair and reasonable standard of comfort." The new legislation concerning the Court, more emphatically than the old, encouraged—indeed compelled—the formation of trade unions in ordinary industries. Consequently the number of trade unionists, which stood at 85,000 in January 1936, had reached the figure of 200,000 by January 1938.

Labour had come to power, not merely with the support of the workers, but also with that of many small farmers, and the special innovation to assist them was rationalized marketing, involving the assumption of ownership by government of all dairy produce intended for export, purchased at a price guaranteed for the year. Similarly rationalization was carried out in the dairy industry through the amalgamation of cheese and butter factories, the zoning of areas of supply and the shutting down of inefficient units. Government action was feasible in this industry because the units were co-operatively owned, and when once the Labour administration had won the sympathy of the co-operative organizations, the road to reform was open.

Such are only a few of the principal measures of projected change, but they are sufficient to indicate that Labour began where the Liberals of the nineties had left off. It set New Zealand once more moving on the road to social democracy. Much controversy has taken place as to what this experiment means. Is it socialism? Some supporters of Labour are glad to answer in the affirmative, but the term "socialism" is more often applied to it by its enemies than by its friends, and for good reason. The average elector of New Zealand has as much abhorrence for what he considers the name "socialism" covers as, say, the average farmer of Ontario. It is, as a fact, simply democracy. It is democracy in action under, for the time being, peculiar pressures—especially the pressure of workers and small farmers joined once more in common political agreement. There is, however, no ground to assume that this political agreement would extend to the creation of a completely socialized economy; there is every reason to believe that it would not, unless under the coercion of conditions that we cannot at present readily visualize.

Unfortunately for Labour's experiment, the mid-thirties were different from the nineties. New Zealand's daring little venture in guaranteeing prices for farm products and its attempts to insulate itself from the commercial hurricanes of the outer world seemed small things when that world contained Stalin, Hitler and Mussolini. The extension of reform towards social democracy was more difficult and perilous than its beginning in an earlier period. It was, for example, reasonably feasible for the industrial arbitration court established in the nineties to guarantee wages in the face of an upward drift of prices; but to guarantee prices to primary producers in the late thirties as a step to general stabilization was a different matter. It was certainly destined to lead to a succession of additional and far-reaching economic controls far beyond those already attempted. However, the harsh strains of war have intervened, and New Zealand's attempt to extend its empiric social democracy must at the time of writing revert to other ends than simply the standard of living. But there is no doubt that the recommencement of energetic reform in 1935 was an event of major significance for the democracy of the dominion, and for the history of democracy in the Commonwealth. From the start then made, social experimentation in the future is likely to proceed.

South Africa stands apart from all the other dominions, for its problems of political solidarity have only a partial resemblance elsewhere, and in no other dominion does democracy work in an atmosphere of such intense and singular passion. Two facts deeply influence the political life of the Union: the clash in culture and interest between white men and black, and the conflict of nationalities (usually called races in South Africa) within the white population. Turning to the first of these, I choose the word "clash" deliberately. It is not extravagant, because behind the relations between the races is a genuine struggle of cultures for survival. That of the white man is the stronger, but the strength is not such as to breed a sanguine attitude of mind, a fact clearly enough illustrated when one considers the figures of population in the last census. The Bantu represent 68.8 per cent., mixed and coloured 8 per cent., Asiatic 2.3 per cent., people of European extraction a little over 20 per cent. The Bantu, numerically the dominant race, are unlike the natives of other dominions in possessing a relatively rugged social vitality. They have not dwindled before the advance of the white man's civilization, partly no doubt because in their reserves they have remained somewhat intact from the more devastating impact of that civilization; and partly because their large initial numbers have enabled them to withstand the shocks of cultural conflict better than scantier populations, such as the Australian aborigines. Their place of future power in the social structure of South Africa is secure, and their retarding influence upon the attempt to create a South African democracy must continue.

On the relation of the native to the politics and society of the white man, there have been two divergent policies with zealous exponents since Great Britain, in 1815, acquired the Cape: *assimilation* and *segregation*. Assimilation is generally the goal of the liberal and the humanist. Its ideal is expressed in the words of Rhodes: "equal rights for all civilized men irrespective of colour", implying that the franchises of the Bantu in the State should widen as his civilisation advances. It is never contended, except by the fanatic, that equality of rights can immediately be recognized, but rather that the course of legislation on racial contacts must be plotted in relation to the principle of an ultimate equality, instead of on the basis of the principle that for all calculable time the white man must retain his dominance to the negation of equality. In brief, complete assimilation is the remote, not the immediate goal.

Segregation is perhaps best defined in language long known in South Africa as "the policy of keeping the Kaffir in his place", and his place is not assumed to be one of equality with the white man, or of competition with him whether in the economic, political or social sphere. This is the official policy of the Union today.

Assimilation as an ideal aim has since 1910 formally met defeat. But for obvious reasons the logic of segregation is not inexorably followed out in all spheres of the economy; it would involve too sharp a wrench in the white man's life. It would imply the withdrawal of the cheap Bantu labour from South African farms (the last census shows that over one-third of the Bantu are so situated), the native "pick and shovel" men from the mines of the Rand, and the numerous domestics, male and female, from homes all over the Union. Consequently farmers, mine owners, and householders may use the blessed word segregation (it is something of an emotional symbol useful to the politician), but they mean segregation only in so far as it does not affect their cheap labour supply, or only in so far as it affects the labour supply of somebody other than themselves.

Similarly in politics, segregation, if carried to its logical conclusion, might mean a ring of self-governing native states on the borders, with some thrust into the heart of the Union—a prospect that few Afrikanders could view with composure. Tribute is paid to complete segregation as an ultimate and remote goal; especially is such tribute paid when political leaders are addressing working men, who of all classes are usually, for obvious reasons, keen for the policy. But the policy is actually implemented only where no powerful interests of the white South African are destined to suffer. In most spheres, therefore, it is only partial, and would perhaps better be described as "differentiation", designed to lessen the danger of race mixture and to keep within bounds competition between the races in the interest of the white labourer. A certain amount of such partial segregation has existed for a long time; it is illustrated in the reserves where a large part of the native population lives according to its traditional culture; it is also revealed in the maintenance of native townships set apart from those of Europeans in the suburbs of the cities, and in the placing of native huts on the farms apart from the dwellings of the white proprietors.

In matters of government the present policy of partial segregation is reflected in the legislation of 1936. It is impossible here to go into the complicated subtleties of the enactments of that year. It is sufficient simply to mention that the old native and coloured franchise of the Cape Province, provided originally by the constitution of 1854, is modified greatly to conform to the principle of segregation. Those entitled to the franchise are placed on separate electoral rolls, with the power of electing three white representatives to the assembly and three to the provincial council. Outside the Cape Province, the natives have no power to elect members to the assembly but through electoral colleges choose four white representatives for the senate. A truer reflection of the segregational principle was the establishment of a Natives' Representative Council, on which natives sit and exercise powers mainly of advice; e.g., they pass upon bills affecting the native population and may recommend such bills to parliament and the provincial councils. Here perhaps is the beginning of a separate representative system for the natives of the Union, the starting-point of a true segregational structure in government. It does not, however, disguise the fact that only to a limited degree does the native govern himself. Rather he is under an elaborate system of administrative law framed by white men. Only in a very restricted sense does he share in the democracy of the Union. His people of six-odd million are, for political purposes, a dependent class; a passive portion of the community. A political serfdom, qualified by some measures of local government on the native reserves, would be a reasonably accurate description. If and when the native ceases to be a political serf and achieves a genuine citizenship on segregationalist principles, South Africa will present the picture of an even more singularly strange state; a state split into two sections along the lines of colour, and perhaps the victim of interminable clashes between the two communities on economic and social issues. It is clear that this is not a prospect likely to awaken enthusiasm in South African minds, and it is little wonder that, except for the speculations of a few intellectuals, South African thought on the native issue does not project into the future; it dwells content with the sufficiently difficult problem of the present.

The system devised for the native affects the methods of ruling the white minority as well as the black majority. It is obviously difficult for a government to depend on administrative law in relation to one large sector of social life without being inclined to apply administrative rulings in other sectors. Certainly the Union has much experience of decisions by the departmental mind. Perhaps an even more significant effect on the white man's democracy is the passion of racial fear which the native problem in almost any of its aspects arouses, and which must inevitably hamper the spirit of compromise whereby alone democracy can function well. It is a high tribute to the political capacity of the Dutch and British in South Africa that, in the face of this tantalizing issue of colour, they have succeeded in preserving a parliamentary régime at all. Other countries, facing issues no more grave, have failed.

To the problem of colour is added that of a national cleavage between those of British and those of Afrikander descent (Afrikanders being dominantly of Dutch extraction with French and German elements). This cleavage bears some resemblance to that of French and British in Canada, but for two evident reasons is sharper. The history of actual physical conflict between the two nationalities is much more recent, for it is less than forty years since the conclusion of the Second Boer War. Men still alive—indeed many in parliament today—were on opposing firing lines. Bitter memories still linger of women and children in concentration camps. Of almost equal importance is the fact that the two nationalities are territorially less segregated than in Canada—an advantage in the long run, since the merging of the two becomes easier, but in the interval disturbing issues like that of bilingualism are made more acute.

The key, of course, to the frictions between the two white peoples is found in the character of Afrikaans nationalism, which has been expressed in political form by the Nationalist Party since 1912. It is the national-ism of men who believe that a policy of racial reconciliation would sacrifice the Afrikander, render him less conscious of and interested in his own culture and traditions, and throw him into the vortex of im-perialism, with all the sinister meaning of imperialism to the Boer. Such a cause has made an inevitably powerful appeal to the conservative farmer of the platteland. For generations he has been taught by his leaders (not least by the predikants of the Dutch Reformed Church) to distrust and to fear British influence, whether peaceful or otherwise; for it was a force which threatened to change the deep customs of his life and to destroy that rugged independence developed within him from the day that his forefathers had begun to trek across the coastal mountain ranges and stubbornly to fight their way north. "Nothing", wrote Olive Schreiner more than forty years ago, "so indicates the dogged, and almost fierce strength of the South African Boer as his unique conservatism"; and she added the remark, probably as valid today, that "in him the seventeenth and even remnants of the sixteenth century are found surviving as among few peoples in Europe."[1] This conservatism has been the product of isolation. If ever there was a case of the frontier fashioning social ideas, it is found in the influence on the Boer of isolation on the veld. To hold fast to his culture was the basic condition of his physical survival, surrounded as he was by crude and harsh conditions of life. He learned the lesson so well that today his deep conservative impulses are the foundation of an uncompromising nationalism. He learned to plant his foot, and stand still.

The practical issues emphasized by the Nationalists have generally concerned the relations of the Union with the Empire. In the years previous to the last war, consistent hostility characterized their attitude towards measures of imperial co-operation. "Imperial-

---

[1] Olive Schreiner, *Thoughts on South Africa*, 256.

ism", said General Hertzog in that period, "is only important to me when it is useful to South Africa." But that remark itself suggested a concession, since to many of his rabid followers any connexion with the Empire must be evil. They looked with suspicion upon the attendance of South African ministers at imperial conferences, and news that Botha, while attending the Conference of 1911, had been guest of His Majesty in full court dress, including silk stockings, had only to be repeated in the platteland to create bitter feeling. Botha's silk stockings "gradually assumed the shape of a symbol of national treason." Preferences on the import of British goods were resented, while a policy of encouraging British immigrants was deplored as a threat to the numerical position of the true Afrikanders. The most advanced ideal of the Nationalists was a completely independent republic, and, for this end, some of them instigated the brief rebellion of 1914. When they assumed power in 1924, the republican ideal was replaced by that of a kind of "crowned republican status" within the Empire, but since the commencement of the present war the shibboleth of the republic has once more appeared. It is doubtful how far one must attach significance to it as a practical political idea. The "republic" is another of these effective symbol words. Its social implications are seldom carefully analyzed by those leaders who use it; they are often little interested in its material implications. For them it is sufficient that its usage evokes a response from the back-veld farmer or the young college student, euphemistically described as an intellectual. It stirs the emotions of the nationalist Afrikander, for through a republican status he assumes that he would achieve a psychological emancipation from the stigma of conquest in the past. But the hard-headed politician—a species found in South Africa as in other dominions—while he may use this effective symbol word, knows that the British South Africans do not want a republican status and are still politically strong enough to veto it, as organized labour did in 1925. Doubtless in time the British South Africans may become apathetic. They may cease to care much about the imperial connexion, and then the patient Afrikander will win. He may then get his republic, and at last be free.

This absorption in the concepts of an intense nationalism—the nationalism of a small and very conservative people—has naturally restrained that type of liberalism which has been a dynamic faith in democracy elsewhere in the British Commonwealth. Inspiration is frequently sought in the customs of the group rather than in the advancing ideas of modern civilization. I can best illustrate this fact by reference to the parliamentary debate in 1930 on a bill to enfranchise women, when some of the principal Nationalist members strongly opposed the measure, although it was introduced by their leader, General Hertzog. The Minister of Justice, General Kemp, contended like many others that it was "in conflict with the intentions that the Creator had for women."[1] Some speakers inevitably referred to the days of the Voortrekkers, when the women played a heroic part in the settlement and perpetuation of the race without asking for franchises. "If dear old President Kruger", remarked one member, "were on the floor of this

[1] *Debates of the House of Assembly*, 1930, 1532.

House what would he say about women's suffrage."[1] The question was rhetorical. The speaker had no doubt of the answer. The argument of General Smuts that other dominions had long before enacted a female franchise was met with the heated rejoinder: "President Kruger said that we must go to our past. He did not tell us to go to other countries, and look for novelties there."[2] The speaker considered that the measure would plunge the country into darkness. Such views held at the time by a section of the Nationalist Party suggest how little headway liberal doctrine had made against a tenacious traditionalism, whose counterpart elsewhere in the dominions is to be found only in Quebec. It is fair to add, however, that the bill passed into law. The advance of industrialism is gradually breaking down the old structures of thought and social attitudes. But in some matters the pace is not rapid; nor is it likely to quicken greatly because of the permanent and distintegrating issues of colour. Liberalism as a working social creed in South Africa has to contend, as in no other dominion, with a race instinct of immense vitality, and hence perhaps in no part of the British Commonwealth does democracy rest on more precarious social foundations. The impulse for racial protection and survival may prove to be more powerful than the impulse to live according to a concept of liberty.

In conclusion it may be briefly emphasized that the democratic experiments in the dominions to which I referred were made under, and conditioned by, peculiar world circumstances. First, the experiments began,

[1] *Ibid.*, 1630.
[2] *Ibid.*, 2206.

and developed, in a period characterized by the
pax Britannica. From 1840, when roughly the present
British Commonwealth began its growth, to 1914,
British sea power, resting upon wealth and tradition,
policed the trade routes of the world, and controlled
the exits and entrances to the strategic seas. Even
New Zealand, although 12,000 miles from the mother-
state, was not too distant to develop in almost
complete security. Thanks to such freedom from
external danger, British civilization entered upon the
era most distinguished in its history, and the democratic experiments of the dominions were merely
phases—the most vital and significant—of the general
growth in a civilized order. In the later years, dangers
did appear on the horizon, but never assumed a
magnitude profoundly disturbing. The Anglo-Japanese
alliance brought a sense of genuine protection to the
two dominions most isolated and vulnerable. Sheltered
from outside aggression, with few periods of scare,
these communities in their democratic life had little
reason to look outward. They were states in the
happy position of not requiring positive foreign
policies; they were certainly not inhibited in their
internal political development by external perils.

Related to this security is the equally significant
fact that within the same period there was an
unprecedented economic expansion, which affected
especially the English-speaking part of the world, and
as a result of which the primary products from the
dominions found steadily larger markets. Such
expansion made it possible for New Zealand and
Australia to pay readily for their experiments in social
democracy. It eased the frictions in their social

systems. It facilitated that compromise on which democracy rests. It provided the conditions for a generally optimistic social outlook, which coloured democratic experiment. It is not suggested that the democrats of the dominions have been notably extravagant in their expectations of the millenium. Compared with leaders in other countries whom one might mention, they have been sober. But in their sobriety there was an abundance of unmistakable hope. Nature did not seem to be niggardly. The depletion of natural resources was not yet experienced. The nation could be made prosperous, and, with skilful social engineering, all citizens might be made to share in the prosperity. Mere beginnings only, it was believed, were made in building an empire and a commonwealth. The future held out the hope of greater developments (the age produced Rhodes, Chamberlain, Seddon and Laurier); horizons would become brighter and wider.

Since the last war, this period of hope has been changing and disappearing; and since the beginning of the thirties the tempo of change has quickened. A new world has emerged wherein the former rate of rapid economic expansion has been checked and the security of the dominions—especially since the failure of the League—has been challenged as never before. The fact is least recognized in Canada because there the menace seems to be least. Canadians may not, in Senator Dandurand's words, "live in a fireproof house", but at any rate they are immensely more sheltered than the other states of the Commonwealth. And, in addition, their diversified and genuinely vast resources (exaggeration aside) give them a sense of economic security which the two other major dominions cannot equally possess. In view of the world-scene of shifting economic and political forces, it would be foolish to make the most gratuitous of mistakes; viz., prophesy as to the effects of the transformations upon the democratic institutions to which reference has been made. One may only say that while societies seldom turn sharp corners, war perhaps more than any other phenomenon creates the occasion to do so. It is so obvious as hardly to require mention that if British sea power was destroyed as a consequence of the present war, all the dominions would turn a very sharp corner, especially Australia, New Zealand and South Africa. Such destruction would leave every part of the Commonwealth (with the possible exception of Canada—a not too certain exception) at the mercy of Britain's conquerors and their allies. The democratic experiments mentioned above might then become merely history. But this is not a theme to contemplate; let alone elaborate. Even in the more likely and hoped for victory to the allies and the cause of world order, the dominions will have changed greatly under the harsh test of war. Their life inevitably will be determined by the kind of international system which follows, for few countries—owing to their basic nature—will respond more quickly to the course of world history. Prediction need not go further.